Survive the
IB! 2011-2012 Edition

Survive the IB! :
An essential student's guide to the international Baccalaureate Diploma

© *2010-2011 Nathan Taber , Layline Publishing*
Book & Cover design by Nathan Taber
Editing by Michaella Latkovic

Please note: The terms **"IB"**, **"International Baccalaureate"**, and any IB syllabus information included here are **not** under any free license and remain property/trademark of the IBO.

The material in this book has been developed independently of the International Baccalaureate®, which in no way endorses it.

These materials are reproduced here for personal study purposes only.

For updates, links, helpful resources, and more; visit www.survivetheib.com

First Printing: June 2011

ISBN-13: 978-1-463-61209-2

ISBN-10: 1463612095

**Dedicated to all of the teachers, family, and
friends that have made this dream a reality.**

Thank You

for Michaella & Corrie

"The International Baccalaureate aims to develop inquiring, knowledgeable and caring young people who help to create a better and more peaceful world through intercultural understanding and respect. To this end the organization works with schools, governments and international organizations to develop challenging programmes of international education and rigorous assessment. These programmes encourage students across the world to become active, compassionate and lifelong learners who understand that other people, with their differences, can also be right."

—International Baccalaureate Mission Statement

Survive the
IB! 2011-2012 Edition

written and compiled by:
Nathan Taber

About This Book

This is your field guide to the International Baccalaureate (IB) Diploma program. You may be one of many IB candidates spending much of their time the way that I did: in the dark, fumbling for a hand-hold in what seems to be an insurmountable academic mountain.

Ask around and you will find that many students in the IB diploma program have a very incomplete idea of how the program works.

Nobody seems to really understand what all the strange European lingo means and exactly what it takes to get your diploma.

Whether you are a freshman trying to decide if the IB is right for you or a senior who is waist deep in the academic fray, this guide has been designed to answer all of your questions.

It is a reference to those who are lost, a compilation of facts and advice taken from my personal experience in getting an IB Diploma, IB teachers and program coordinators, as well as the thoughts and insights of fellow IB students.

The IB program does not have to be a death trap. There are many diploma candidates who get good grades, go to sleep every night, have a social life, participate in activities outside of school, and go on to top universities.

To help every IB candidate get the most out of themselves and the diploma program; I have done my best to show clearly and exactly how this program works.

Besides a thorough overview of each component of the diploma progarm, I have included worksheets, a glossary, and a list of resources so that you can easily find what you need in order to get your diploma.

Some of the realities of IB are unavoidable. There is no way to completely avoid stress in the diploma program. There will be times when you feel overwhelmed and out of control.

Pick this book up when you do. A lot of stress in IB comes from not knowing what exactly you need to do or having too much to do. To help ease the load, I have included sections devoted to organization, effectivity, and stress management.

My hope is that this book will provide you with an invaluable reference and guide to the IB program, ultimately making your experience with this one-of-a -kind program enjoyable, exciting, and world-class.

What's New

For the 2011-2012 school year, the International Baccalaureate Program is undergoing some major revisions. Beyond the normal cycle of course updates, several key components of the diploma program have been changed in order to better meet the needs of candidates.

Groups 1 and 2

The biggest changes are happening in the language program. In order to better accommodate multi-lingual candidates, the Language A1 and Languages A2 courses are no longer being taught.

For Group 1, three new courses take the place of Language A1. Literature, Language and Literature, and Literature and Performance each provide new options for more candidates.

Groups 3 and 6

For 2011-2012, the course in Economics has a new, updated syllabus and two new courses: World Religions and Dance.

So what does this mean?

All of these changes are for courses that are *started* this fall. Any courses continuing from last year (2010-2011) will not be changed.

If this is your first year in IB, everything in this book will be accurate for you. If this is your second year in IB, ask your coordinator or contact us through www.survivetheib.com if you are not sure about what course information is right for you.

About the IB

IB stands for International Baccalaureate or more specifically the International Baccalaureate Organization. The IB is a nongovernmental organization that is a subset of UNESCO. Founded by teachers from the International School of Geneva in 1968, the International Baccalaureate is still headquartered in Geneva, Switzerland.

The IB produces and organizes educational curriculums for primary, middle, and elementary schools worldwide. As of 2010, there are 2,820 registered IB World Schools® globally, with 1,072 located in the United States.

The complete IB curriculum consists of three separate programs for different age groups. Respectively, these are the Primary Years Program (PYP), Middle Years Program (MYP), and the Diploma program. The IB Diploma is the one offered in high schools and it is the focus of this guide.

The IB Diploma program is a 2-year intensive high school educational curriculum aimed at giving high school students around the world a competitive and internationally standardized learning experience.

The curriculum structure encourages a higher standard of education and features specially trained teachers, standardized in-class assignments and testing, and an intense academic atmosphere.

One of the major benefits of the IB being an internationally standardized program is that US students receiving an IB diploma can competitively apply to international schools as well as gain college credit for their coursework in many domestic universities.

Ultimately, the IB diploma program is a valuable departure from the traditional US & Canadian high school honors curriculums. Its intense focus on international standardization, balanced learning, and fair evaluation provides the framework for a more challenging and complete education than is routinely offered to students in most North American schools.

As you begin...

Please take caution when using this manual.

While every effort has been made to make the material in this text up to date and as accurate as possible, the IB is constantly re-evaluating and updating their requirements and procedures for candidates.

I have done my best to clearly identify sections of the guide that contain potentially time-sensitive material and the appendix is stocked with links to resources that have updated information.

Additional resources, links, and IB news can be found on our website:

www.survivetheib.com

If there is any question to the accuracy of the program overviews and requirements for matriculation in any particular section, please refer to the resources listed in the appendix or the IB faculty at your school.

If you have questions about any aspect of the IB program, want to share your story, or have any suggestions on how the book might be improved, please write us at:

feedback@survivetheib.com.

We are always looking for ways to improve and revise.

Your comments, questions, and suggestions are highly valued!

Contents

The Basics

Survival

Afterwards

Appendix

The Basics

"If you teach a man anything,
he will never learn"
                    - Bernard Shaw

1   ***Orientation***

The IB program is a little bit different from any other high school curriculum. While there is a lot to learn, the IB is not focused on teaching facts and dates. Rather the goal is to teach you **how to learn**.

You read that right. The International Baccalaureate is not consuming and difficult because you need to know a lot. While memorization, research, and writing dozens of papers is not easy, this is not the most challenging part of the IB.

The most difficult aspect to the IB diploma is improving and changing your mind set about who you are, the way you go to school every day, and the way that you do your homework every night.

Everything you know is wrong

I know that having to re-evaluate everything you know about how to go to school can be like a cold splash of water to the face.

However, the IB is only torture if you make it so. The program is difficult and demanding, and even though many students give up every year, just as many students receive their diplomas.

The secret to beating the IB Diploma lies in your attitude.

If you approach the IB Diploma program as a huge monster ready to swallow you whole, that is exactly what will happen to you. Soul and all. Change your attitude, however, and you will find the entire experience bearable, maybe even enjoyable.

The goal of the IB Diploma program is to create and nurture students who think, people who can look at problems in new and creative ways and use information to come to unique conclusions. This program is designed to create students who do not just know facts, but how to go out and dig up new answers.

By opening this book, you have already taken the initiative to become one of these students. Use this guide until the pages are ripped and torn. The IB is not here to suck your life away, it is here to shape you into a super student - someone ready to tackle the world and take life head on.

Profile of an IB Candidate

Before you can get what you want out of the International Baccalaureate, it is important to know what the IB wants out of you. The International Baccalaureate Diploma program is focused on developing students who are:

Inquirers	Principled
Critical Thinkers	Caring
Communicators	Open-minded
Risk Takers	Well-balanced
Knowledgeable	Reflective

Keep these ten traits in mind. Every learning objective in each IB course directly relates back to them. By mastering each trait, the diploma program will come naturally to you, and you will find yourself with less stress, more time, and better grades.

Two Pathways

There are two pathways for students who take IB classes: certificates or the full diploma.

Certificates

The simplest option for students is the certificate program. Students can attend and test in their choice of IB courses and receive certificates in each respective subject. Schools have different requirements on taking these classes but for the most part, to take an IB class and receive a certificate simply means enrolling in the course and taking the appropriate exam(s).

The benefit of the certificate program is that you can take IB classes, but without any commitment beyond any particular courses you sign up for.

In most schools, a student who is only taking classes for certificates must still complete their school's state mandated requirements for graduation.

The IB Diploma

The other option for students is the full IB Diploma program. Students who attempt a full diploma complete classes in all areas of the IB program; including the Theory of Knowledge (TOK), Creativity, Action, and Service hours (CAS), and an Extended Essay project (EE).

In most schools, students must apply to the diploma program and are accepted by the school based on criteria that includes past academic performance and their personal goals in the program. Requirements for admission are set at the discretion of the school and IB program coordinator.

The focus of this guide is on the full IB Diploma program. While the information here is still intrinsically valuable for any student, I have written this assuming that you are attempting a full diploma.

The Bilingual Diploma

This one is for the real achievers. Candidates who successfully complete courses in multiple languages are eligible to receive a bilingual diploma. Additionally, receiving a bilingual diploma allows candidates to take courses from groups 3 and 4 in a language that is not their first.

Bilingual diplomas are awarded for completing:

- Two Language A courses

- A group 3 or 4 subject taken in a language other than the candidate's Language A

- An extended essay in a group 3 or group 4 subject written in a language other than the candidate's Language A.

For more details, talk to your IB coordinator.

Information from http://www.ibo.org/diploma/recognition/guide/slidef.cfm

4

Benefits of the IB

The International Baccalaureate Diploma program offers numerous benefits for diploma candidates.

The intangible benefits of the diploma program are countless. Going through the IB is boot camp training in how to critically think and reason. It is a crash course in academic excellence.

Attempting an IB diploma teaches you how to work under pressure as well as how to organize your thoughts, activities, and time during high school to a level that many people will not achieve during their entire lives.

The IB diploma program has numerous tangible benefits as well. In my mind, this is the best college prep program out there. Many others, including top colleges and universities agree that the IB diploma is one of the best college prep programs in the world.

More and more, colleges and universities are recognizing the International Baccalaureate for developing intellectual, educated, motivated, and generally well-prepared people.

Many US and Canadian colleges will give credit based on a student's IB scores. At some universities, students can earn up to what is equivalent to a year of college credit for their work in the International Baccalaureate.

For my IB diploma, I earned 30 credits (equivalent to two-thirds of a year of study) towards my college degree before I even got the key to my dorm room. While my friends had to take college required classes like English 101 during freshman year, I could take whichever classes I wanted to.

Several of my classmates from IB have even used their credits to get out of college a year early, or to acquire two degrees in half of the time that most people take.

Additionally, the IB program gives students the opportunity to attend university abroad. International schools are often hesitant to accept normal US high school grades because they see them as inconsistent and unreliable. The IB Diploma, however, is internationally recognized and can offer reliable gateway to attending top schools outside of your home country.

2 ***Elements of the IB***

From the outside, the IB diploma program can seem to be inherently complicated, confusing, and downright intimidating.

For most of my IB career I had a very fuzzy picture of how the program actually worked. Never knowing why something was happening, or what was going to be due when, I was often left stumbling blindly through course after course.

Many students want to know: why does the IB program have to be so complex? Well, the answer is that the IB is designed to be complete. When you understand the program as a whole, it becomes much easier to see where each piece fits.

Structure of Diploma Program

The diploma program is made up of six subjects. In order to receive an IB diploma, candidates must successfully complete one course in each subject area:

> Group 1: Primary Language
> Group 2: Secondary (Foreign) Language
> Group 3: Study of Individuals and Society
> Group 4: Experimental Sciences
> Group 5: Mathematics
> Group 6: The Arts

Additionally, all candidates for the IB diploma are required to:

- Submit an extended essay in one of the IB subject groups

- Complete the course in Theory of Knowledge (TOK)

- Fulfill requirements for CAS (creativity, action, service) hours

Classes and Assessment

Each course in the diploma program is structured around a common curriculum. While the given curriculums for some courses are more complete and specific than others, each one includes a list of topics that are expected to be covered as well as learning objectives for each subject.

Beyond this, IB teachers are specially trained to develop and implement courses according to standards and requirements set out by the IB.

This means that while the exact course curriculum may vary from school to school, around the globe, IB courses are the same. IB Biology at Colegio Peruano Britanico in Lima, Peru is essentially the same as IB Biology at Cleveland High School in Portland, Oregon.

One of the key differences between IB and normal high school classes is how courses are graded. Scoring for IB courses relies solely on assessment. That is, assignments and homework do not count towards receiving an IB diploma.

IB courses are graded based on two types of assessments: internal and external. Generally, a course will have one internal assessment project and one two- or three-part external assessment.

Internal Assessments

Internal assessments are assignments, projects, or portfolios that reflect work done during a class.

The internal assessment is graded by the course instructor who evaluates the work according to requirements set up by the IB. After the assessments for the course are graded, the instructor will send their grades, along with several samples of the work from the class to the IB.

Trained and impartial evaluators then re-grade the sample work and adjust the scores for the entire class accordingly. This means that while the course instructor grades internal assessments, the IB moderates this grading so that any errors or bias in an instructor's grading can be adjusted for.

External Assessments

The external assessment is an exam which covers every section of the curriculum and takes place at the end of the course.

In the Northern Hemisphere, IB exams take place over a period of several weeks in May. In the southern hemisphere, IB schools conduct their exams in November.

Each external assessment is composed of several "papers", or sections of the exam, which test different sections of the course. Each paper contains questions in one of several different formats: multiple choice, essay, short-answer, etc.

The time given to complete each paper can vary from 45 minutes to more than 2 hours.

The papers for a single subject may be tested over multiple days giving students time to prepare for each specific paper in advance.

The external assessment is administered at the school and all completed papers are sent to various locations around the globe to be officially evaluated by the IB.

These assessments are very heavily standardized and the IB expects that every student in each IB school around the world will take the exact same version of a respective exam.

I took my HL chemistry exam without a periodic table of the elements because one school in South Africa did not receive copies in time for their examinations and tested without the periodic table. Because they didn't get the periodic table for their exam, neither did we.

Grades

IB courses are graded on a scale from 1-7. Each grade is a combination of the scores from the external and internal assessments. The weight each assessment carries may vary depending on the course.

The standards for grading in the IB are different from those used in the majority of North American schools. They are intensively quantitative and each course is graded on an exact and strict mark scheme.

Grades are assigned on a scale from 1-7:

7 Excellent performance
6 Very good performance
5 Good performance
4 Satisfactory performance
3 Mediocre performance
2 Poor performance
1 Very poor performance

On a more quantitative level, each question carries a certain number of points. Each exam is then scored out of this total number of possible points. So in effect, a score 7 is roughly equivalent to a 100 percent, a score of 5 equivalent to 80 percent, etc.

TOK and the Extended Essay are graded on a scale of A-E:

A Excellent performance
B Good performance
C Satisfactory performance
D Mediocre performance
E Elementary performance

In many North American schools, only an A or a B is seen as acceptable marks and students are graded on the idea that "good" work deserves an A. The IB however, grades on philosophy that "good" work is average, and thus merits at most a C or B. In most cases, only excellent work will receive a B while a piece must be truly outstanding to merit an A.

To this end, scoring a 7 on an exam or an A on your extended essay is not common and scoring this high is a sign that you have greatly exceeded expectations for the assessment.

Content

Even though IB courses are evaluated by examination, the curriculum takes deliberate steps to ensure that the course is not taught solely 'for the exam'. You will still receive homework and grades for your classes that are required for your regular high school diploma.

It is still important to do daily homework. Not only will homework ensure that you pass high school, it is one of the best ways to thoroughly learn a subject in preparation for the IB exam.

HL & SL courses

Each IB course is offered at one of two levels: higher lever (HL) or standard level (SL).

Of the courses studied in IB, three to four must be completed at the higher level (HL) of study, and no more than three courses may be completed at the standard level (SL) of study.

HL and SL courses differ in three major ways:

First, HL courses are taught over significantly more time than SL courses. Each HL course is allotted 240 teaching hours while an SL course is allotted 150 hours. This means that HL courses are taught over two years while SL courses take place in one.

The second major difference lies in the extra depth and detail that is covered by HL courses. Due to there being much more time to learn the subject, HL courses explore their subjects at greater depth and with additional topics when compared to the SL courses.

To this end, students in an HL course are expected to develop higher level skills in a particular topic than students in an equivalent SL course.

The third major difference between HL and SL courses is reflected in the course assessments. External assessments at the HL level often include additional papers to cover the extra material, and the papers themselves tend to be longer and more in-depth than SL papers.

While the requirements for the internal assessment tend to be the same for both HL and SL course levels, the internal assessments from HL classes are graded with the expectation that students understand the material and the assignment at a higher level.

Timeline

The Pre-IB

The first step of your IB career will probably be taking pre-IB classes. Depending on your school, there may or may not be a pre-IB program offered. The IB diploma is officially a two-year program, however due to its rigor and complexity, many schools elect to ease students into the program with advanced "IB-like" courses during the first two years before starting IB.

The pre-IB program gives you an opportunity to get used to the higher level of class-work demanded in IB before you commit to the full diploma program. If you have taken advanced or honors classes before high school, the pre-IB will not be very different. The two years in pre-IB give you a chance to get to know the IB teachers at your school, take classes in a more challenging environment and to see if you really want to attempt an IB diploma.

For many students the pre-IB is the best time to get used to more challenging courses and to figure out a game plan for their years in the diploma program. In the time before you start the diploma program, the best thing to do is to begin adapting your schedule to focus on school. Do not forget the rest of your life; just try to invest more time in your studies and classes than you did previously.

Do not just complete assignments and write papers; Wikipedia or Google search what you are learning about to get a complete picture of the subject. Do the bonus problems at the back of your math chapters and go to your local library to look up topics that you learn about in other subjects.

While having this little extra knowledge and going the extra distance is not required to pass classes in the pre-IB, the IB diploma program is structured around students who go the extra mile in their studies. Your teachers will be looking for this in pre-IB and even more so once you enter the full diploma program. Set yourself up early for success and you will find it much easier to overcome the many difficulties that IB students face.

Junior Year

Your first year in the IB program will probably be the easiest. You start your HL classes this year and 1-2 SL classes. At the end of the year, you will test in your SL classes only. In the second half of the year, you will start TOK and begin work on your extended essay project.

Senior year

Over the summer, and into your final year in IB, you will work on your extended essay, finishing sometime around December or January. You will finish TOK around the same time and all your CAS requirements must be completed before testing at the end of the year. Having to test in 3-4 HL courses as well as 1-2 SL courses makes this the hardest year in IB.

To see a visualization of this timeline, check out the appendix.

3 ***Subject Groups***

This chapter is designed to walk you through each academic section of the diploma program. Use it as a handy reference whenever you are confused about a course or to figure out exactly what classes to take.

Each part of the chapter gives a brief overview of a particular subject group along with descriptions of the courses offered in that group. Use these descriptions to help you understand the overall focus and goals of any particular course as well as to help in selecting courses to take.

Every school takes a unique stance in which courses they offer for each subject group. Many schools will offer just one or two classes in each subject area, while larger programs may offer several choices.

It is important to remember that the IB program at every school is unique, and that some, if not many of the course options described here may not be available at your school. Like the rest of this manual, use this section as a reference tool and not a definitive guide.

While many of the courses in the diploma program appear similar, every course has its unique quarks and characteristics.

If you need more details about a particular course or subject area, speak to your program coordinator or the teacher at your school that instructs in a particular course. They are great resources for further explanation on some of the more intricate requirements that go along with the diploma program courses.

Do not read straight through this chapter - you will find it incredibly boring. Instead, use the index on the following page and jump directly to whichever course you want to learn more about.

Courses Offered

Group 1
Language A

Group 1 is a very important element of the IB Diploma program. The courses in this subject group focus on teaching candidates how to read, interpret, and write about literature in their native language. Starting in the 2011-2012 school year, Group 1 consists of three courses:

1. Literature

2. Language & Literature

3. Literature and Performance (interdisciplinary)

The main focus of every course in this subject group is on studying and understanding texts which are both native to the language of the course and translated from another language. The goal of this subject is to develop cultural and literary understanding while enhancing communication skills, especially written communication. Unlike other subject groups, the analysis and communication skills taught in Group 1 are essential to success in nearly every other part of the IB Diploma program.

While most Group 1 courses are taught in English in US schools, each of these courses is offered in 80 languages at both the higher and standard levels. A list of available Group 1 languages can be found in the appendix.

If a candidate has a strong background in a certain language which is not offered at their school, it is possible to complete a Group 1 course independently as a school-supported self-taught language. Speak with your IB coordinator for details on this course option.

The assessments in this group can be quite tricky and a list of command words used during the assessments can be found in the appendix. This list can significantly help improve scores by giving a clear understanding of what the questions in this subject group mean and how candidates should properly answer them.

Literature

Language A: Literature is a new course for 2011-2012. It replaces the Language A1 course as a part of the new Group 1 structure that is meant to provide more opportunity and flexibility for primary language instruction in the IB program. Literature is offered both at the SL and HL levels though candidates studying Literature in a school-supported self-taught language complete the course at the SL level only.

Focus

The focus of Literature is to develop literary interpretation and communication skills in a native language. Generally, this consists of reading, orally interpreting, and then writing about literary works chosen from a prescribed list of authors (PLA). Because teachers pick from a list of available works in order to design the course, the specific content and style of each Literature course can vary considerably.

Structure

Literature consists of four parts.

Part 1. Works in translation. This is the study of two (SL) or three (HL) literary pieces that are translated into the native language of the course. These are chosen from a 'prescribed literature in translation' (PLT) list and aim to develop both literary and cultural understanding.

Part 2. Detailed Study. This section consists of reading and performing an in-depth analysis of two (SL) or three (HL) literary pieces. Each of the works is chosen from the PLA and is from a different genre. The goal of this section is to develop literary analysis skills.

Part 3. Literary Genres. Three (SL) or four (HL) works from the same genre are studied. The works are studied comparatively in order to understand the literary conventions and features associated with the particular genre.

Part 4. Options. For both SL and HL classes, three works are freely chosen by the course instructor. Part four gives instructors to the opportunity to spice things up by choosing unique works that they have personal interest in and which allow candidates to reach unique conclusions in light of the other works covered by the course.

Assessment

The assessment of Literature consists of two parts, a written external assessment and an oral internal assessment.

The oral internal assessment is worth 30% of the final mark and consists of two equally-weighted parts:

1. Individual oral commentary. Candidates record an oral commentary and answer questions on an extract from one of the works studied in the second part of the course. For HL candidates, this is followed by a discussion based on a different work chosen from part two.

2. Individual oral presentation based on works studied in the fourth part of the course.

The external written assessment is worth 70% of the final mark and consists of three parts:

Paper 1 consists of a literary analysis on one prose and one poetry passage. SL candidates write in response to two questions while HL candidates write a free-form analysis.

The paper lasts 1.5 hours (SL) or 2 hours (HL) and is worth 20% of the final mark.

Paper 2 is based on part three of the course and consists of three questions for each genre studied. Candidates choose one of these questions and write an essay based on at least two of the works studied in part three.

The paper lasts 1.5 hours (SL) or 2 hours (HL) and is worth 25% of the final mark.

Paper 3 is a written assignment that submitted for external review. The assignment consists of a 300-400 word reflective statement and a 1,200-1,500 word literary essay based on one work studied in part one of the course.

This assignment is worth 25% of the final mark.

Language and Literature

Language A: Language and Literature combines aspects of language study and literary analysis to enable multilingual candidates from varied linguistic backgrounds to effectively complete Group 1 course requirements in a non-native language. This course is new for the 2011-2012 school year and is available at both SL and HL levels.

Focus

Like Language A: Literature, Language and Literature focuses on a study of literary texts in order to develop literary and cultural understanding in addition to analysis skills. A key goal is to help candidates in understanding the meaning created by language and literature. By involving language study in the literary analysis, it is hoped that candidates develop a degree of 'cultural literacy'.

Like other Group 1 courses, Language and Literature consists of reading, orally interpreting, and then writing about literary works chosen from a prescribed list of authors (PLA). Because teachers pick from a list of available works in order to design the course, the specific content and style of each course can vary considerably.

Structure

Language and Literature consists of four parts:

Part 1. Language in cultural context. Various texts from a variety of sources, genres, and media are studied with relation to how language develops in specific cultural contexts and how it shapes identities and the world.

Part 2. Language and mass communication. Various texts are studied with consideration to how language is used in media. Candidates examine different forms of mass media and explore how media uses language and image to communicate.

Part 3. Literature – texts & contexts. Two (SL) or three (HL) literary works are studied. These consist of works written both in the course language and in translation. The goal is to understand how elements of the text are influenced by history, society, and culture.

Part 4. Literature – critical study. Two (SL) or three (HL) literary works are read and analyzed. Detailed analysis of the literature is focused on understanding the meanings and context of a work as well as learning the techniques of literary analysis.

Assessment

The assessment of Language and Literature consists of two parts, a written external assessment and an oral internal assessment.

The oral internal assessment is worth 30% of the final mark and consists of two equally-weighted parts:

1. Individual oral commentary. Candidates record an oral commentary in response to two guiding questions on an extract from one of the works studied in the part 4 of the course.

2. Two further oral activities. One is based on part 1 and one is based on part 2 of the course.

The external written assessment is worth 70% of the final mark and consists of three parts:

Paper 1 consists of a comparative textual analysis on two unseen texts (SL) and two pairs of unseen texts (HL). Candidates write an analysis on one of these.

The paper lasts 1.5 hours (SL) or 2 hours (HL) and is worth 25% of the final mark.

Paper 2 is based on part three of the course and consists of six questions. Candidates choose one question and write an essay based on both of the works studied in part three.

The paper lasts 1.5 hours (SL) or 2 hours (HL) and is worth 25% of the final mark.

Paper 3 consists of three (SL) or four (HL) written tasks, one (SL) or two (HL) of which is submitted for external review. Each task consists of a 200-300 word rationale statement and an 800-1,000 word response to questions regarding material studied in the course.

These tasks are worth 20% of the final mark.

Literature and Performance

Literature and Performance (also known as Text and Performance) is a new interdisciplinary course that fulfills requirements for both Group 1 and Group 6 of the IB Diploma program. While candidates may have some background in critical writing and performance, there are no requirements for experience in either literature, language, or performance for this course. Literature and Performance is offered only at the standard level.

Focus

Literature and Performance is designed to allow candidates to explore and analyze the relationships between literature and theatre. The course combines aspects of theatre performance with critical literary analysis. Candidates are expected to develop a knowledge and understanding of texts from different genres and cultures in terms of their writing and performance potential. Additionally, the course focuses on developing candidates' performance skills as well as ability to clearly understand and assess the works they are performing.

Structure

Literature and Performance consists of three parts.

Part 1. Critical study of texts. At minimum, candidates study one novel, two poetry texts, one play, and a choice of prose or poetry. All texts are read in detail and candidates analyze the different features of each text as well as the meanings behind these features.

Part 2. Exploration of the chosen approach to the text. This is essentially a further exploration of literary features that are selected from those examined in part 1 of the course. Candidates expand their exploration through discussion and casual performance in various spaces.

Part 3. Realization of texts in performance. The final part of the course involves developing and performing a segment of one of the literary works. The final nature of the performance is open-ended and can take on almost any form. The goal of part 3 is to develop performance techniques in conjunction with the literary analysis.

Assessment

The internal assessment for Literature and Performance is worth 40% of the final mark and consists of two parts.

1. A five-minute performance based on one of more of the poetry and prose texts studied during the course. The texts may not be the same as those studied for the external assessment.

2. An individual oral presentation that discusses the performance and the works involved.

The external assessment is worth 60% of the final mark and consists of three parts.

Paper 1 requires candidates to answer one essay question about dramatizing a novel from a choice of three.

This paper is 1.5 hours long and is worth 20% of the final mark.

Paper 2 requires candidates to answer one comparative essay question on works studied during the course from a choice of six.

This paper is 1.5 hours long and is worth 20% of the final mark.

Paper 3 is an externally assessed and independently written assignment that consists of critical analysis on one or more performed extracts from the texts studied during the course. This involves an analysis of the text itself as well as the candidate's performance of it.

The assignment is required to be 1,500-2,000 words long and is 20% of the final mark.

Group 2
Foreign Language

Consistent with the ethos of the IB diploma program, every diploma candidate is required to study a foreign language. Study of a foreign language not only improves and expands linguistic skills, it gives candidates exposure to foreign cultures, traditions, and ideas. The IBO believes that this is critical to the development of any worldly candidate.

All of the group 2 courses, except for Classical Language, are available in a number of languages. As of 2009, over 80 are available (see the appendix for a complete listing).

While the material changes, the demands on candidates as well as the structure and assessment details of each course remain very similar for each language that a course is taught in.

Anticipating that candidates will have different exposure to foreign languages; Group 2 courses range from teaching simple understanding to complex analysis of a foreign language.

Use this guide to make a determination as to what course option best suits you:

Ab Initio: This is a basic introductory language course. It is intended for someone who enters the course with no knowledge of the subject language. As such, Ab Initio is only offered in SL.

Language B: This is for the candidate that wishes to expand their study of a foreign language. It is expected that candidates in Language B have 2-5 years of familiarity and instruction with the subject's language. This is still a learning course, so fluency is not required. If you take Language B, you will not be expected to take other IB courses in any other language besides your primary one (English). It should be noted that in many US schools, the course options for Group 2 may be limited to just several languages in the Language B course.

Classical Languages: This alternative approach to group 2 focuses on the study of either Latin or Classical Greek.

This is the only course where the assessment may not be conducted in the language studied.

SL or HL?

When deciding whether to take the standard or higher level of Language B or A2; it is important to consider your experience and future objectives.

Higher level courses are designed for candidates who have more experience in the target language and intend to study the language significantly beyond the diploma program.

Standard level courses are better suited to those with more limited experience and do not intend on pursuing their language studies at a higher level beyond IB. This is especially true for Language B courses.

Ab Initio

Ab Initio is a secondary language course designed for beginners. This course gives candidates opportunity to a foreign language and culture for the first time. As the course is designed to give an introduction to a new language, it is only offered in the standard level.

Focus

The goal of Ab Initio is on developing candidates to a basic level of communicative competence with the target language as well as exposure to a culture that was previously unknown. The course seeks to do this by developing the four primary language skills: listening, speaking, reading, and writing.

Assessment

The course assessment consists of 30% oral work in the form of an internal assessment and 70% as an external written assessment.

The oral assessment is conducted in two parts.

- The first part is conducted as a short individual interview with the teacher and is worth 15% of the final mark.

- The second part is an interactive oral activity worth 15% of the final mark. This can take many forms including a whole class debate, group or pair project, or role playing assignment.

The written assessment consists of two papers. Note that dictionaries are not permitted during testing.

The first paper usually takes about 1.5 hours and is worth 40% of the final mark. This paper is designed to test your ability in understanding and assessing information from various texts in the subject language.

The paper presents four texts followed by a number of text-handling exercises. Usually the final text will require a short written response. The texts increase in difficulty as the examination continues.

The second paper is a written response made up of two different prompts. The first prompt is a short answer (more than 60 words), while the second is an extended response (more than 120 words).

This paper takes about 1.5 hours and is worth 30% of the final mark. It is important to use at least the minimum required number of words when answering the prompts to receive the maximum possible marks.

Language B

Language B is designed for candidates who have some experience learning a foreign language and the development of skills at a higher level than Ab Initio.

For many candidates in the United States, this is the main Group 2 course offered.

Language B is offered in over 80 languages and in both the higher and standard levels. Like Ab Initio, the general outline of each language course is the same, but the syllabus will differ for each specific language. (See the appendix for a complete list of languages offered)

Focus

Language B focuses on candidates further developing and acquiring the four primary language skills: listening, speaking, reading, and writing.

The course is designed to take candidates from understanding basic vocabulary and syntax of a language to competency in conversation and literature. As well, candidates are exposed to the culture and customs relevant to the language studied.

Language B candidates are expected to:

- Communicate clearly, fluently, and effectively in a range of situations

- Understand and use a range of vocabulary

- Understand and analyze moderately complex written and spoken material

- Show understanding and sensitivity to the culture(s) related to the language studied

On par with normal IB standards, candidates at the higher-level are expected to meet these expectations with a greater level of competency than those taking the course at the standard-level.

Structure

Language B focuses on acquiring and developing language skills through listening to the language being spoken, speaking in the classroom, reading, and writing assignments.

In both SL and HL classes, three core subject groups covered:
1. Communication and media
2. Global Issues
3. Social Relationships

Additionally, two additional subjects from five options are covered:
- Cultural diversity
- Customs and traditions
- Health
- Leisure
- Science and technology

HL candidates additionally study two works of literature in the course language.

Assessment

For Language B courses, the internal assessment is oral and is worth 30% of the final mark. The external assessment is written and is worth 70% of the final mark.

The oral component is similar for both HL and SL courses and consists of two parts.

The first part is a ten-minute individual oral presentation and discussion with the teacher that is based on the two course segments studied as options. The individual oral is worth 20% of the final mark.

The second part is an interactive oral activity that is based on the three core course segments. It consists of three classroom activities and is worth 10% of the final mark.

The externally assessed written component is also the same for both HL and SL courses and consists of a written assignment and two examination papers, each 1.5 hours long.

Paper 1 is worth 25% of the final mark.

This paper consists of text-handling exercises that are based on the core subjects.

Paper 2 is worth 25% of the final mark.

SL and HL candidates complete one writing exercise of 250-

400 words from a choice of five.

Additionally, HL candidates write a 150-250 words assignment based on one of the core subjects.

The written assignment is worth 20% of the final mark for both SL and HL candidates.

SL: A written exercise based on a text reading from one of the three core subjects. The exercise is 300-400 words along with a 100 word rationale.

HL: A creative writing assignment based on one of the literary texts studied during the course. The assignment must be 500-600 words plus a 150 word rationale.

Classical Language

Classical Language studies are very different from other group 2 courses. In Classical Languages, candidates study ancient Greek or Latin and the culture of the Greek or Roman civilization.

While Greek and Latin are two separate languages, like other language courses, they share the same syllabus and assessment procedures. Candidates who study Classical Language are expected to have prior experience and a basic familiarity with the texts, grammar, and syntax of Latin or ancient Greek.

Focus

While the course has a significant amount of study devoted to the cultural achievements and historical developments of these ancient peoples, there is a strong belief that the works examined are most valuable when studied in their original form. As such, the course maintains its focus on the linguistics of the respective civilization.

Classical Language aims to give candidates a deeper understanding of the subject language in a range of situations. As well, the course encourages cultural understanding and awareness, developing the appreciation for classical texts, and providing candidates a basis for further study of the subject language and culture.

Structure

Classical language courses have two parts. The biggest difference in syllabus between HL and SL courses is the breadth of the subjects studied, number of texts studied, and the number of hours devoted to the course as a whole.

- The first part is a study of the language. This is the guided study of one or two prescribed authors in order to develop language skills. Candidates are eventually required to translate into English a passage written by that author.

- The second part is a detailed study of two genres of work in the original language chosen from five prescribed genres. Supplementary readings given in translation may also accompany this study.

Assessments

For Classical Language, the internal assessment is worth 20% of the final mark, while the external assessment is worth 80% of the final mark. For both HL and SL candidates, the assessment requirements are very similar.

For the internal assessment, candidates complete one of three options as part of the course:

1. A research dossier consisting of a collection of source materials relating to a topic in classical history, literature, language, religion, art, archeology, mythology, or some aspect of classical culture. The dossier should be annotated to demonstrate connection and understanding.

2. An oral presentation that consists of a passage read aloud in the respective language and accompanied by a written commentary.

3. A translation of English, Spanish, or French prose or verse into Latin or classical Greek accompanied by a written commentary.

The external assessment consists of two papers:

The first paper is worth 35% of the final mark and consists of a translation of one or more specified parts from an unseen passage by a specified author.

For HL candidates, this paper lasts 1.5 hours and for SL candidates this paper lasts 1.25 hours.

The second paper is worth 45% of the final mark and consists of questions that are based on ten extracts from studied works. There are two extracts from each genre studied.

HL candidates answer questions on four extracts from two genres and the examination lasts 2 hours.

SL candidates answer three questions from two genres and the examination lasts 1.5 hours.

Group 3
Individuals and Societies

The courses in Group 3, Individuals and Societies focus on the interactions between people and their environments in different times and places. The group is more commonly known as the social sciences and it is made up of nine distinct subject courses.

While candidates are only required to study one subject in this group in order to receive an IB diploma, many schools offer several subjects from this group. This provides candidates opportunities for more focus in similar subject areas and to take courses that are outside the normal realm of a high school education.

There are nine available courses in Group 3:
• Business and management
• Economics
• Geography
• History
• Information Technology in a Global Society
• Philosophy
• Psychology
• Social and Cultural Anthropology
• World Religions
• Environmental Systems & Societies

Each subject in Group 3 may be studied at the HL or SL level. The flexibility and course options in this group often lead candidates to take group 3 subjects at a higher level, or to take one course as SL and another as HL.

These courses have a strong focus on human society's impact on itself and the environment. This gives many of the courses in Group 3 a strong connection to the Theory of Knowledge course.

Indeed, the IB believes that this group is a fundamental part of the diploma program and during each course, a number of questions and issues may arise that are excellent subjects for discussion and analysis on a broader, more philosophical scale in TOK.

Business and Management

The Business and Management coursework focuses on giving the candidate an understanding of how business organizations function from both economic and managerial standpoints. The course examines the decision making processes of businesses and how these decisions affect the business and impact the world.

The focus of Business and Management is leading candidates to an understanding about the structure and daily functioning of different types of businesses, decision making processes used by these businesses, and the implications of business activity in global markets.

Goals

The goals of the Business and Management course are to:

- Promote the importance of exploring business issues from different cultural perspectives

- Encourage a holistic view of the world of business

- Enable the candidate to develop the capacity to think critically about individual and organizational behavior

- Enhance the candidate's ability to make informed business decisions

- Enable the candidate to appreciate the nature and significance of change in a local, regional and global context

- Promote awareness of social, cultural and ethical factors in the actions of organizations and individuals in those organizations

- Appreciate the social and ethical responsibilities associated with businesses operating in international markets.

Structure

There are five to six topics that are covered in the Business and Management course. Topics 1-5 are covered by both HL and SL classes while topic 6 is covered only by HL classes.

Topic 1: Business organization and environment
Topic 2: Human Resources
Topic 3: Accounts and Finance
Topic 4: Marketing
Topic 5: Operations Management
Topic 6: Business Strategy

Assessments

The internal assessment is completed during the normal progression of the Business and Management course and is worth 25% of the final mark.

The HL internal assessment consists of a research proposal and written report based on a research question that either addresses an issue facing an organization, or range of organizations, or analyses a decision to be made by an organization or range of organizations. The proposal must be 200-300 words and the written report is 1800-2000 words.

Generally, the research proposal is written during the first year of the course and the report is completed during the second year of the course.

The SL internal assessment consists of a written assignment based on the application of tools, techniques and theory to a real business situation or problem. This assignment is 1000-1500 words.

The examinations for businesses and management consist of two papers and are very similar for both HL and SL.

Paper 1 is worth 40% of the final mark for HL candidates and 35% of the final mark for SL candidates. It is based on a case study which is provided and studied in class before the examination. The case study and examination questions address all of the subjects which are studied during the course.

While the paper 1 is similar for both HL and SL candidates; HL candidates answer four structured questions in three parts, while SL candidates answer three questions in two parts.

For HL candidates, paper 1 lasts for 2.25 hours, for SL candidates it lasts 1.25 hours.

Paper 2 is worth 35% of the final mark for HL candidates and 40% of the final mark for SL candidates. The paper covers all of the subjects studied during the course and consists of the candidate answering three of 5 structured questions in two parts.

The paper lasts 2.25 hours for HL candidates and 1.75 hours for SL candidates.

Economics

Coursework in Economics is aimed at providing an understanding of basic micro and macroeconomic principles as well as international and developmental economics. The course focuses on the application of these principles in everyday business and international governments.

Candidates split their time between learning theoretical economic principles and the applications of these principles to real-world business. Additionally, the course seeks to develop candidates' ability to apply economic theories to a range of circumstances and situations, analyze information regarding economic theories and situations, and evaluate these concepts from different perspectives.

Structure

The course aims to give candidates a very broad overview of the major topics in Economics. These are covered in four general sections during the course:

1. Microeconomics
2. Macroeconomics
3. International Economics
4. Developmental Economics

This syllabus structure is essentially the same for both HL and SL classes.

Assessments

The internal assessment in Economics is similar for both the HL and SL levels and consists of a portfolio made up of three commentaries on different economic subjects. Each commentary must be 650-750 words and is based on different sections of the course as well as published extracts from news/media pieces. The only restriction is that sources may not be from television or radio broadcasts.

For both SL and HL courses, the internal assessment is worth 20% of the final mark.

The external assessment for Economics consists of two papers for SL candidates and three papers for HL candidates.

Paper 1: An extended response paper with two sections.

Section A is a response to one question on microeconomics from a choice of two.

Section B is a response to one question on macroeconomics from a choice of two.

Paper 1 is worth 40% (SL) or 30% (HL) of the final mark and lasts for 1.5 hours.

Paper 2: A data response paper with two sections.

Section A is a response to one question on international economics from a choice of two.

Section B is a response to one question on development economics from a choice of two.

Paper 2 is worth 40% (SL) or 30% (HL) of the final mark and lasts for 1.5 hours.

Paper 3 is for HL candidates only. The paper draws from all syllabus material, including the HL extension material and consists of two questions chosen from a selection of three.

Paper 3 lasts 1 hour and is worth 20% of the final mark for HL candidates.

Geography

Geography is a course that holds middle ground between the human and physical sciences. The course is unique among Group 3 as the coursework examines social interactions as well as scientific methods and observations relating to geography.

Candidates study physical geography, topography, population, urbanization, agriculture, economic growth, and natural (environmental) hazards.

In some ways, this is a flagship course for the IB as it allows candidates to integrate many different subjects while gaining an objective and worldly view of both human interaction and physical science.

Structure

The coursework in Geography is structured around 3 to 5 themed sections.

HL and SL classes both complete four core subject groups:
1. Populations in Transition
2. Disparities in wealth and development
3. Patterns in environmental quality and sustainability
4. Patterns in resource consumption

The second part of the course consists of two (SL) or three (HL) additional subjects which are chosen from a list of seven.
5. Freshwater issues and conflicts
6. Oceans and their coastal margins
7. Extreme Environments
8. Hazards and disasters – risk assessment and response
9. Leisure, sport, and tourism
10. The geography of food and health
11. Urban Environments

The third section of the course is completed only by HL classes. It consists of the study of seven topics.
12. Measuring global interactions
13. Changing space – the shrinking world

14. Economic interactions and flows
15. Environmental change
16. Socio-cultural exchanges
17. Political Outcomes
18. Global interactions at the local level

Finally, both SL and HL courses participate in geographical field work which forms the basis for the second part of the internal assessment.

Assessments

The internal assessment for Geography consists of a report based on their work and findings from the fieldwork section of the course. The work can be on any component of the syllabus and must be a at most 2,500 words.

The internal assessment is worth 20% of the final mark for HL candidates and 25% of the final mark for SL candidates.

The external examinations consist of two papers for SL and three for HL.

Paper 1 is worth 25% of the final mark for HL candidates and 40% of the final mark for SL candidates. The paper is based on the first section of the course and consists of two parts.

In the first part there are a series of short answer questions.

In the second part there is one extended response question.

Paper 1 lasts 1.5 hours for both SL and HL candidates.

In Paper 2, Candidates answer two (SL) or three (HL) questions from the second part of the course. For each section, candidates choose to answer one structured question out of a choice of two.

Paper 2 is worth 35% of the final mark and lasts 1.3 hours for SL candidates, 2 hours for HL candidates.

Paper 3 is for HL candidates only. The paper is based on the fifth section of the course. Candidates choose one essay question from three provided options.

Paper 3 lasts for 1 hour and is worth 20% of the final mark.

History

IB History is a comprehensive examination of the interactions between individuals and societies in a historical context. The course approaches history as an exploratory subject for that does not necessarily present definitive answers; instead seeking to develop the attitude that, in historical evaluation, content and methodologies are not always correct and their study mandates a toleration and familiarity with uncertainty.

To this end, IB History seeks to expose candidates to both primary historical sources and the evaluations of historians while expanding their knowledge and appreciation of the topics studied. The course also focuses on developing candidates' abilities to extrapolate understanding and critically evaluate historical events.

Structure

IB History is taught in two sections for both SL and HL, with a third section added for HL classes.

The first section covers several introductory topics in the subject area, while the second section covers five more advanced fields of study. The third HL section is equal in size to the second section and focuses broadly on the historical aspects of one chosen area of the world.

There are two different paths that the course may take. One path focuses on the History of Europe and Islamic World, while the other focuses on 20th century world history. It should be noted that often these two courses are known separately as 'Islamic History' and 'History' rather than being seen as one course with two paths.

The course for the History of Europe and Islamic world consists of:

Section 1:
  1. The origins and rise of Islam c500-661
  2. The kingdom of Sicily 1130-1302

Section 2:

1. Dynasties and rulers
2. Society and economy
3. Wars and warfare
4. Intellectual, cultural and artistic developments
5. Religion and the state

Section 3:

1. Aspects of the history of medieval Europe and Islamic world

The course for 20th century World History consists of:

Section 1:

1. Peacemaking, peacekeeping – international relations from 1918 to 1936
2. The Arab-Israeli conflict 1945-1979
3. Communism in crisis 1976-1989

Section 2:

1. Causes, practices and effects of war
2. Democratic states – challenges and responses
3. Origins and development of authoritarian and single-party states
4. Nationalist and independence movements in Africa and Asia and post-1945 Central and Eastern European states
5. The Cold War

Section 3:

1. History of Africa
2. History of the Americas
3. History of Asia and Oceania
4. History of Europe and the Middle East

Assessments

The internal assessment for History consists of a historical investigation on any area studied in the course. The investigation is about 20 hours of work.

For HL candidates, the assessment is worth 20% of the final mark, for SL candidates it is worth 25% of the final mark.

The external examinations consist of two papers which are similar for both SL and HL, with a third paper added for HL candidates.

Paper 1 is worth 20% of the final mark for HL candidates and 30% of the final mark for SL candidates. The paper consists of four short answer/structured questions that are based on the material studied in the first section of the respective course.

Paper 1 lasts for 1 hour for both HL and SL candidates.

Paper 2 is worth 25% of the final mark for HL candidates and 45% of the final mark for SL candidates. The paper is made up of two extended response questions based on the second section of the course studied.

Paper 2 lasts for 1.5 hours for both HL and SL candidates.

Paper 3 is for HL candidates only and is worth 35% of the final mark. This paper consists of three extended response question which cover the entire course studied.

Paper 3 lasts for 2.5 hours.

Information Technology in a Global Society

Often abbreviated as ITGS, Information Technology in a Global Society focuses on the study and evaluation of the impacts that information has on people and their societies.

The course aims to familiarize candidates with information technology (IT) systems, teaching the structure of such systems and enabling them to evaluate the widespread social impact of these technologies both on themselves and the society around them.

This course is different from computer science in that it focuses on the social impact of technology and the overall structure of IT systems, where computer science focuses on a detailed study of how these systems function, both logically and internally.

Structure

There are three sections (also known as strands) studied in ITGS. All three sections are covered by both HL and SL candidates. Additionally, HL candidates study two chosen topics an additional extension segment for each respective section and an annually issued case study.

Section 1: Social and Ethical Significance focuses on the social and ethical considerations linked to IT developments. There are 12 topics studied:

1. Reliability and Integrity
2. Security
3. Privacy and anonymity
4. Intellectual Property
5. Authenticity
6. The digital divide and equality of access
7. Surveillance
8. Globalization and cultural diversity
9. Policies
10. Standards and protocols
11. People and machines
12. Digital citizenship

The HL extension for section 1 links social and ethical considerations in IT to two chosen topics and a case study which is used in the course

43

Section 2: Application to Specified Scenarios studies the application of IT to six general scenarios:

1. Business and employment
2. Education and training
3. Environment
4. Health
5. Home and leisure
6. Politics and Government

The HL extension for section 2 studies scenarios based on real life situations in the two HL extension topics and a case study which is given by the IB each year.

Section 3: IT Systems studies the terminology, concepts, and tools relating to IT developments. This section studies 9 topics:

1. Hardware
2. Software
3. Networks
4. The Internet
5. Personal and public communications
6. Multimedia/Digital media
7. Databases
8. Spreadsheets, modeling and simulations
9. Into to project management

The HL extension for section 3 studies three additional topics:

1. IT systems in organizations
2. Robotics, artificial intelligence and expert systems
3. Information systems specific to the issued case study

Assessments

The internal assessment for ITGS is the same for both HL and SL candidates. The assessment consists of candidates developing an original IT product for a specified client. In doing this, candidates produce the product along with documentation of 2000 words or less supporting their development.

The internal assessment is worth 30% (SL) or 20% (HL) of the final mark.

The external assessment consists of two papers for SL candidates and three papers for HL candidates.

For SL candidates, paper 1 is worth 40% of the final mark and consists of the candidate answering three of five structured questions designed to asses all three parts of the course.

Paper 1 lasts 1.75 hours for SL candidates.

For HL candidates, paper 1 is worth 35% of the final mark and consists of the candidate choosing four out of seven structured questions in three sections:

Two of three questions on any of the core subject topics

One of two questions based on topic 10 from section 3: "IT systems in organizations"

One of two questions based on topic 11 from section 3: "Robotics, artificial intelligence and expert systems"

Paper 1 lasts 2.25 hours for HL candidates.

Paper 2 is the same format for both HL and SL candidates and is worth 30% (SL) or 20% (HL) of the final mark. The paper consists of a written response to one unseen article.

Paper 2 lasts for 1.25 hours.

Paper 3 is for HL candidates only and is worth 25% of the final mark. This paper consists of four questions on the case study which is examined during the course.

Paper 3 lasts for 1.25 hours.

Philosophy

Philosophy in the IB program seeks to enable candidates to develop their thinking on issues that are complex, challenging, and important for human society. The course deals with fundamental questions that individuals and societies have asked throughout history, guiding candidates to relate their philosophical understanding to personal and social life as well as other disciplines.

Philosophy also aims to teach candidates how to critically examine their own experiences and biases, as well as formulate logical and rational philosophical arguments.

The study of philosophy can take two paths, study of the development of philosophy and "doing" philosophy. The IB course takes a solid stance towards "doing" philosophy. This means that IB Philosophy focuses candidates on learning philosophy through active philosophical discussion and exploration rather than studying how others think.

As such, candidates are expected to develop the abilities to reason and construct logical arguments, providing a starting point from which candidates can develop into independent thinkers.

Structure

IB Philosophy is divided into several sections. The first section consists of the study of three different themes.

The first theme is studied by all classes and is based around the question:

"What is a 'human' being?"

Beyond this core theme, classes study one (SL) or two (HL) of eight optional themes:
1. Grounds of epistemology
2. Theories and problems of ethics
3. Philosophy of religion
4. Philosophy of art
5. Political philosophy

6. Non-Western traditions and perspectives
7. Contemporary social issues
8. People, nations and cultures

The second section of the course studies several prescribed texts and is completed by both HL and SL classes.

The third section of the course is centered on completing the internal assessment.

The fourth part of the course is studied only by HL classes only and is a study of an unseen text. This is used as a learning tool and in preparation for the external assessment.

Candidates are required to develop a philosophical response after being presented with a text to which they have no previous exposure.

Assessments

Internal assessment in Philosophy is a critical analysis of non-philosophical material. For HL the internal assessment is worth 20% of the final mark, for SL candidates it is worth 30% of the final mark.

The external assessment in Philosophy consists of three written papers for HL candidates and two for SL candidates. The first two papers take the same form for both HL and SL candidates.

Paper 1 is worth 40% of the final mark for both groups. The paper has two sections:

Section A requires the candidate to answer one of two provided questions based on the core theme: "What is a 'human' being?"

Section B requires the candidate to answer one essay question for each optional theme which was studied during the course.

HL candidates answer two essay questions, SL candidates answer one.

Paper 1 lasts 2.5 hours for HL candidates, 1.75 hours for SL candidates.

Paper 2 is worth 20% of the final mark for HL candidates and 30% of the final mark for SL candidates. The paper requires candidates to write one essay question out of two presented for each prescribed philosophical text.

Paper 2 lasts 1 hour for both HL and SL candidates.

Paper 3 is for HL candidates only and is worth 20% of the final mark. The paper presents one unseen text and requires candidates to write a response to it. Paper 3 lasts for 1.5 hours.

Psychology

IB Psychology is an integrated examination of the interaction between cognitive, biological, and social influences on behavior. The goals of the course include enabling candidates to learn how psychological knowledge, develop and applied as well as to develop a greater understanding of who they are.

To this end, the course in IB Psychology focuses on teaching the concepts and skills of basic psychology as well as critical thinking and experimental investigation.

Structure

The course for is made up of four sections. HL candidates study all of the sections, while SL candidates only study three.

Part 1 is the core section of the course. It covers three major topics:

- The biological level of analysis
- The cognitive level of analysis
- The sociocultural level of analysis

Part 2 consists of several topics beyond the scope of part 1. Depending on the course, not every topic may be covered.

- Abnormal Psychology
- Developmental Psychology
- Health Psychology
- Psychology of human relationships
- Sport Psychology

Part 3 is covered by HL candidates only and covers qualitative research methodology.

Part 4 is covered by SL and HL candidates and consists of an introduction to experimental research methodology. This section directly leads to the internal assessment.

Assessments

For both HL and SL candidates, the internal assessment in Psychology consists of a simple experimental study conducted by the candidate and an accompanying written report.

For HL candidates, the internal assessment is worth 20% of the final mark, for SL candidates it is worth 25% of the final mark.

The external assessment consists of three papers for HL candidates and two papers for SL candidates. The first two papers are the same for both levels while the third paper is for HL candidates only.

Paper 1 is related to the first part of the course and is worth 35% of the final mark for HL candidates and 50% of the final mark for SL candidates. The paper consists of two sections:

Section A: three questions.

Section B: one essay question selected from a choice of three.

Paper 1 lasts for 2 hours.

Paper 2 is related to the second part of the course. The paper is worth 25% of the final mark for both HL and SL candidates. HL candidates answer two essay questions from a choice of 15; SL candidates answer one essay question from the choice of 15.

Paper 2 lasts for 2 hours for HL candidates, 1 hour for SL candidates.

Paper 3 is for HL candidates only and is worth 20% of the final mark. The paper consists of three questions based on an unseen text from based on the third part of the course.

Paper 3 lasts for 1 hour.

Social and Cultural Anthropology

Social and Cultural Anthropology is a comparative study of culture and society. Anthropology in IB focuses on teaching anthropological perspectives and methodologies as well as helping candidates to develop critical reasoning and analysis with regard to anthropological theories and observations of characteristics of societies and cultures.

Structure

There are five distinct components that make up the course. SL candidates complete parts 1,2, and 3 while HL candidates complete parts 1,2,4, and 5, skipping parts 2 and 3.

Part 1 focuses on the question "What is anthropology?" in three topics:
1. Core terms and ideas
2. Construction and use of ethnographic accounts
3. Methods and data collection

Part 2 focuses on social and cultural organization in eight topics:
1. Individuals, groups and society
2. Societies and cultures in contact
3. Kinship as an organizing principle
4. Political organization
5. Economic organization and the environment
6. Systems of knowledge
7. Belief systems and practices
8. Moral systems

Part 3 consists of an exercise in observation and critique and is completed by SL candidates only.

Part 4 covers theoretical perspectives in anthropology and is completed by HL candidates only.

Part 5 consists of anthropological fieldwork and is completed by HL candidates only.

Assessments

For HL candidates, the internal assessment is worth 25% of the final mark and consists of a report on the fieldwork completed in the fifth section of the course.

For SL candidates, the internal assessment is worth 20% of the final mark and consists of two activities:

1. A one-hour anthropological observation accompanied by a written report.

2. A critique of the initial written report.

The external assessment consists of two papers for HL and SL candidates with an additional third paper completed by HL candidates.

Paper 1 consists of three questions based on an unseen text and covers the entire scope of the course.

The paper is worth 20% of the final mark for HL candidates and 30% of the final mark for SL candidates. It lasts for 1 hour.

Paper 2 consists of two essay questions based on the second part of the course which are chosen from 10 presented options.

The paper is worth 35% of the final mark for HL candidates and 50% of the final mark for SL candidates. It lasts for 2 hours.

Paper 3 is for HL candidates only and consists of one essay question chosen out of five which are based on theoretical perspectives of anthropology.

The paper is worth 20% of the final mark and lasts for 1 hour.

World Religions

For the 2011-2012 school year, World Religions is a new course in Group 3 and is offered at the standard level. In the context of this subject group, World Religions studies the interactions between humans and spirituality. The course involves a systematic and analytical study of the beliefs and religious practices around the world through classroom learning and local experience.

The goal of World Religions is to connect elements of individuals and societies with other IB program elements such as the Theory of Knowledge in an objective and open-minded study of religion.

Structure

World Religions is composed of two parts.

Part 1: Introduction to World Religions studies five world religions with the guiding questions of (1) What is the human condition?, (2) Where are we going?, and (3) How do we get there?

Part 2: In-depth Studies examines the rituals, sacred texts, doctrines/beliefs, religious experience, as well as ethics and moral conduct of two world religions. These elements are studied both through classroom research and optional visits to local religious institutions.

Assessment

The internal assessment consists of a written analysis based on an investigative study of a chosen religion which is conducted through a visit, interview, or research.

The analysis must be 1,500-1,800 words and is worth 25% of the final mark.

The external assessment is composed of two papers.

Paper 1 is based on the Part 1 of the course and is composed of nine response questions, each of which deals with a different world religion. Candidates must answer five of the questions.

Paper 1 lasts for 1.25 hours and is worth 30% of the final

mark.

Paper 2 is an in-depth analysis based on Part 2 of the course. It is composed of fourteen essay questions of which candidates answer two.

Paper 2 lasts for 1.5 hours and is worth 45% of the final mark.

Environmental Systems and Societies

Environmental Systems and Societies is transdiciplinary course that covers subject groups 3 & 4: Individuals and Societies and the Experimental Sciences. The course was designed to combine the techniques and knowledge from both subject groups.

Because it spans two subject groups, this course allows candidates to fulfill the requirements for both groups, allowing candidates the freedom to take another course from a different group.

Environmental Systems and Societies aims to merge the gap between these two subjects by promoting an understanding of environmental processes though analysis of environmental issues at a scientific level and the impacts of these issues at a human level.

Additionally, candidates study the roles of technology in creating and solving environmental problems as well as the roles of international collaboration in solving these issues and the controversies that they provoke and surround them.

The course focuses on a holistic approach to understanding the subject and specifically focuses on the concepts of systems and sustainability.

For now, Environmental Systems and Societies is only offered at SL; there is no HL option for this course.

Structure

There are seven main topics covered during the course:

1. Systems and models
2. The ecosystem
3. Human population, carry capacity and resource use
4. Conservation and biodiversity
5. Pollution management
6. The issue of global warming
7. Environmental value systems

Assessments

The internal assessment for Environmental Systems and Societies is worth 20% of the final mark and consists of a series of practical and fieldwork activities.

The activities follow a practical scheme of work (PSOW) which is planned by each course instructor and is designed to reflect on each part of the syllabus. Candidates carry out a range of investigations and document their work through the ES/PSOW form.

The external assessment is worth 80% of the final mark and consists of two papers.

Paper 1 is worth 30% of the final mark and is made up of short answer and data-based questions. Paper 1 lasts for 1 hour.

Paper 2 is worth 50% of the final mark and is made up of two sections: A and B. Paper 2 lasts for 2 hours.

   A. Candidates analyze a range of data relating to a specific case study, coming up with reasonable and balanced judgments of the situation presented based on the data presented.

   B. Candidates answer two structured essay questions from a choice of four.

Group 4
Experimental Science

The courses in the experimental sciences group 4 focus on teaching candidates not only the core subject in each course, but also the scientific method, how scientists work and communicate with each other, and the international repercussions of scientific knowledge.

Group 4 aims to develop candidates' abilities to reason and synthesize scientific information while enabling them to use and apply the knowledge, techniques, and methods of science to develop experimental and investigative scientific skills.

To accomplish this, each course spends approximately ¾ of its hours teaching the material and ¼ of the hours in giving practical experience to the candidates.

There are four subjects offered as experimental science courses:

1. Biology

2. Chemistry

3. Physics

4. Design Technology

The structure of group 4 subjects is markedly different than other IB subjects. The teaching segment of the courses generally consists of two parts.

The first part of the course is made up of the core topics in the discipline.

The second part of the course is made up of two topics which are selected from a list of optional topics by each class. This means that every group 4 class is unique as the syllabus is extremely flexible for a major portion of the course.

Like in other IB courses, there is more coursework for HL candidates and thus HL classes in group 4 will cover more of these optional topics than SL classes. As well, HL classes cover additional topics in the core section of a course.

The practical segment of the courses is split between working on investigations and the group project.

It should be noted that Environmental Systems and Societies, the IB program's first transdisciplinary subject may fulfill the requirement for group 4. The structure and requirements of the course are covered in the TSL section at the end of this chapter.

Group 4 Assessments

Unlike courses in other subject groups, all experimental science classes have the same structure for their internal and external assessments.

Internal Assessments

The internal assessment is worth 24% of the final mark for all courses except design technology where the internal assessment is worth 36% of the final mark.

For Biology, Chemistry, and Physics; the internal assessment is composed of a mixture of short and long-term investigations conducted during the practical segment of the course. The investigations focus on the assessment of practical skills as well as teaching and reinforcing theoretical concepts taught in the course.

Normally, the course instructor designs a practical scheme of work outlining the investigations carried out for the internal assessment though investigations may also be designed by candidates as long as they fulfill the assessment criteria.

In design technology, the internal assessment is composed of a design project which also makes up much of the coursework. More details of the design project are presented in the section on design technology.

External Assessments

The externally moderated assessments for the experimental sciences are composed of three papers for both HL and SL classes.

Paper 1 is worth 20% of the final mark for both HL and SL candidates.

For HL candidates, the paper consists of 40 multiple choice questions based on core topics. Approximately 20/40 of these questions are based on the additional HL materials studied in the core section. For SL candidates the paper consists of 30 multiple choice questions based on the core topics.

Paper 1 lasts 1 hour for HL candidates and .75 hour for SL candidates.

Paper 2 is worth 36% of the final mark for HL candidates and 32% of the final mark for SL candidates. The paper is made up of two sections which cover the core topics as well as the additional core topics for HL candidates.

- Section A consists of one data-based question and several short-answer questions.

- Section B consists of two extended response questions chosen from four (HL candidates) or three (SL candidates) options.

Paper 2 lasts 2.25 hours for HL candidates and 1.25 hours for SL candidates.

Paper 3 is worth 20% of the final mark for HL candidates and 24% of the final mark for SL candidates. The paper consists of several short answer questions for each of the two options studied. HL candidates additionally answer one extended response question for each of the two options.

Paper 3 lasts 1.25 hours for HL candidates and 1 hour for SL candidates.

The group project

A unique part of the group 4 coursework is the group project. The group project is designed to bring together candidates from every science subject at a school as they work together to investigate a common topic or problem.

In smaller IB schools, all science candidates will work together on a single project while in larger schools the candidates may be split into several groups. Some aims of the group project include showing that many problems and concepts in science are multidisciplinary and to foster cross-discipline understanding in candidates.

To this end, the focus in the group project is on the process of the investigation rather than its product.

Biology

Biology in the IB focuses on teaching a carefully selected body of facts while developing understanding of four basic biological concepts:

1. Structure and Function
2. Universality vs. diversity
3. Equilibrium within systems
4. Evolution

Structure

There are 6 core topics covered by both HL and SL classes:

1. Statistical Analysis
2. Cells
3. The chemistry of life
4. Genetics
5. Ecology and evolution
6. Human health and physiology

For HL classes, there are 5 additional topics which are covered at greater depth:

7. Nucleic acids and proteins
8. Cell respiration and photosynthesis
9. Plant science
10. Genetics
11. Human health and physiology

For the optional section of the course, HL and SL candidates study two options from those available for their level.

Options A-C are available only to SL classes:

A. Human nutrition and health
B. Physiology of exercise
C. Cells and Energy

Options D-G are available to HL and SL classes

D. Evolution
E. Neurobiology and behavior
F. Microbes and biotechnology
G. Ecology and conservation

Option H is available only to HL classes:

H. Further human physiology

Chemistry

IB Chemistry focuses on teaching fundamental chemical principles, splitting its time between academic study and the development of practical and investigative experimental skills.

In experiments and assessments, chemistry candidates use the IBO provided chemistry data booklet which gives necessary facts and figures that are used by all candidates to draw conclusions from their academic and experimental observations.

Structure

It should be noted that while the topics covered in Chemistry are presented in a certain order here, teachers are encouraged to arrange the course as it suits them. Therefore your course will contain all of the following elements, though not necessarily in the order presented.

There are 11 core topics covered by HL and SL classes:

1. Quantitative Chemistry
2. Atomic structure
3. Periodicity
4. Bonding
5. Energetics
6. Kinetics
7. Equilibrium
8. Acids and bases
9. Oxidation and reduction
10. Organic Chemistry
11. Measurement and data processing

In HL classes, an additional 9 topics are studied at a deeper level:

12. Atomic Structure
13. Periodicity
14. Bonding
15. Energetics
16. Kinetics
17. Equilibrium

18. Acids and Bases
19. Oxidation and reduction
20. Organic chemistry

For the optional section of the course, HL and SL candidates study two options from the 7 available.

These options are the same for both HL and SL classes:

1. Modern analytical chemistry
2. Human biochemistry
3. Chemistry in industry and technology
4. Medicines and drugs
5. Environmental chemistry
6. Food chemistry
7. Further organic chemistry

Physics

IB Physics seeks to develop the skills of candidates in the traditional and practical skills of physics as well as in mathematics and theoretical understanding.

Additionally, the course aims to give candidates a world-perspective of physics and its underpinnings to human scientific and social advancement.

Structure

There are 8 core topics studied by HL and SL classes:

1. Physics and physical measurement
2. Mechanics
3. Thermal physics
4. Oscillations and waves
5. Electric currents
6. Fields and forces
7. Atomic and nuclear physics
8. Energy, power, and climate change

HL classes also cover an additional 6 topics in greater depth:

9. Motion in fields
10. Thermal Physics
11. Wave Phenomena
12. Electromagnetic induction
13. Quantum physics and nuclear physics
14. Digital technology

For the optional section of the course, HL and SL students study two options from those available for their level.

Options A-D are available only to SL classes:

A. Sight and wave phenomena
B. Quantum physics and nuclear physics
C. Digital technology
D. Relativity and particle physics

Options E-G are available to HL and SL classes

E. Astrophysics
F. Communications
G. Electromagnetic waves

Options H-J are available only to HL classes:

H. Relativity
I. Medical physics
J. Particle physics

Design Technology

Design Technology is a unique course in group 4. It is an ideal departure from the traditional science course, especially for candidates who struggle with or dislike experimental sciences.

The course focuses on teaching candidates the materials, processes, and roles of designs and designers. This includes teaching how designers must consider material, political, social, and economic factors which affect peoples' priorities when designing a product.

Candidates are taught how to evaluate existing products and analyze situations so that they can suggest appropriate improvements.

Additionally, Design Technology maintains a strong emphasis on giving candidates the experience of designers and as such is a central part of the course is the design project where candidates collaborate to design and produce an object of their own design.

Structure

Design Technology consists of two major course segments: Theory and Practical work.

The Theory segment consists of two parts, with some additional topics covered in HL courses.

The core consists of seven topics:
1. Design Process
2. Product innovation
3. Green Design
4. Materials
5. Product development
6. Product design
7. Evaluation

HL courses cover 5 additional topics:
8. Energy
9. Structures
10. Mechanical Design
11. Advanced Manufacturing Techniques

12. Sustainable development

Following the core subjects, SL and HL candidates choose one of five options to study:

Option A: Food science and technology

Option B: Electronic product design

Option C: CAD/CAM

Option D: Textiles

Option E: Human factors design

The practical work segment of Design Technology focuses on applying the theory learned in the first part of the course. For both SL and HL candidates, this section consists of three parts, the main difference between the two levels being that HL candidates spend more time working on the investigations and design project.

1. Investigations
2. Design Project
3. Group 4 project

Group 5
Mathematics and Computer Science

Mathematics and Computer Science is made up of several courses in mathematics and one in computer science. In order to receive a diploma, candidates must complete at least one course in mathematics.

Computer Science is considered to be an elective course and does not fulfill the group 5 requirement, though it may fulfill the requirements for group 6.

There are four different mathematical courses available:
1. Mathematical Studies (SL)
2. Mathematics SL
3. Mathematics HL
4. Further Mathematics (SL)

Computer science is offered at both the HL and SL levels.

Each course in mathematics is designed to meet the needs of a particular type of candidate based on their preferences and future aspirations in mathematics.

You should consider what you already know about mathematics and choose carefully when deciding which course to take.

Additionally, every course in mathematics has a list of topics that are assumed to be prior knowledge (PK). Candidates do not need to know everything on PK list before taking the course, but should know every item before taking the exams. I have included these lists with each subject as appropriate.

All the courses in IB Mathematics aim to develop logical, critical and creative thinking as well as expanding candidates' knowledge of mathematical concepts and principles.

The courses also seek to enable candidates to employ and refine their abilities of abstraction and generalization and are targeted at candidates who wish to study mathematics in depth.

Mathematical Studies

Mathematical Studies is a standard level course which takes a more casual and informal approach to mathematics than other courses.

Designed for candidates who have a limited or varied background in studying mathematics; the course is ideal for candidates who do not anticipate a serious future study of the subject or who's interests lie outside of the field.

It is intended to build confidence and encourage the candidates' appreciation of the subject while equipping them with applicable knowledge of basic mathematical subjects.

Mathematical Studies is unique in that it focuses on encouraging logical thinking rather than relying on the memorization and comprehension of algorithms and formulae.

The course is taught only at the standard level.

Presumed Knowledge

It is assumed that candidates taking mathematical studies have a background in the following mathematical topics:

- Basic use of the four operations of arithmetic, using integers, decimals and simple fractions, including order of operations.
- Prime numbers, factors and multiples.
- Simple applications of ratio, percentage and proportion.
- Basic manipulation of simple algebraic expressions including factorization and expansion.
- Rearranging formulae.
- Evaluating formulae by substitution.
- Solving linear equations in one variable.
- Solving systems of linear equations in two variables.
- Evaluating exponential expressions with integer values.
- Order relations $<, \leq, >, \geq$ and their properties.
- Intervals on the real number line.

Structure

The course is made up of 8 topics:
1. Introduction to the graphic display calculator
2. Numbers and algebra
3. Sets, logic and probability
4. Functions
5. Geometry and trigonometry
6. Statistics
7. Introductory differential calculus
8. Financial Mathematics

Assessment

The internal assessment in mathematical studies is worth 20% of the final mark.

The assessment consists of a project which allows candidates to use the information and skills learned in the course as well as see develop their understanding and appreciation of mathematics as a discipline.

The project is a written work based on personal research involving the collection, analysis and evaluation of data. The subject of the project is up to the candidate as long as the focus is on mathematical content rather than simple research and presentation of facts.

The external assessment is made up of two written papers, each of which is worth 40% of the final mark and lasts for 1.5 hours.

Paper 1 consists of 15 short-response questions which are based on the whole course.

Paper 2 consists of 5 extended response questions based on the whole course.

Mathematics SL

Mathematics SL, also known as Mathematical Methods, is an approach to mathematics for candidates who anticipate the need for a solid mathematical foundation in their future studies.

The course is broad and demanding as it seeks to introduce important mathematical concepts through the development of mathematical techniques.

The goal of Mathematics SL is to introduce these important concepts in a coherent and comprehensible manner so that the candidate is enabled to better understand the mathematical underpinnings in fields such as chemistry and economics.

Structure

There are 7 topics which are studied:

1. Algebra
2. Functions and equations
3. Circular functions and trigonometry
4. Matrices
5. Vectors
6. Statistics and probability
7. Calculus

Assessments

The internal assessment for Mathematics SL consists of a portfolio made up of two pieces of work. Each piece of work must be based on a different topic from the course and one of two tasks:

1. Mathematical investigation
2. Mathematical modeling

Both types of tasks must be represented in the portfolio.

The internal assessment is worth 20% of the final mark.

The external assessment for Mathematics SL is made up of two written papers. Each paper is worth 40% of the final mark and lasts for 1.5 hours.

Both papers have two sections, A and B and all of the questions are based on the entire course.

Paper 1 does not permit use of a calculator.

A.   Short response questions

B.   Extended-response questions

Paper 2 requires a graphic display calculator (GDC)

A.   Short-response questions

B.   Extended-response questions

Mathematics HL

Mathematics HL is an advanced course which is best suited to candidates who have a solid background in mathematics and are considering including mathematics in their studies beyond the IB program.

This is a very intensive mathematics course, you should consider your background, final marks, and aspirations in mathematics before taking it.

Structure

Mathematics HL is made up of two sections. In the first, candidates study 7 core topics and in the second section the class selects one topic to study from four options. If you wish to study an optional topic which is not covered in your particular math HL class, consider taking the Further Mathematics course in addition to math HL.

The core topics are:
1. Algebra
2. Functions and equations
3. Circular functions and trigonometry
4. Matrices
5. Vectors
6. Statistics and probability
7. Calculus

The four optional topics are:
1. Statistics and Probability
2. Sets, relations and groups
3. Series and differential equations
4. Discrete mathematics

Assessments

The internal assessment for Math HL consists of a portfolio made up of two pieces of work. Each piece of work must be based on a different topic from the course and one of two tasks:
1. Mathematical investigation
2. Mathematical modeling

Both types of tasks must be represented in the portfolio and the internal assessment is worth 20% of the final mark.

The external assessment for Math HL consists of three papers. Paper 1 and 2 are made up of material from the core section of the course while paper 3 covers material from the option studied.

Paper 1 is worth 30% of the final mark and does not permit use of a calculator.
   A. Short response questions
   B. Extended-response questions

Paper 2 is worth 30% of the final mark and requires a graphic display calculator (GDC)
   A. Short-response questions
   B. Extended-response questions

Paper 3 is worth 20% of the final mark and requires a graphic display calculator. It consists of several extended response questions.

Further Mathematics

IB Further Mathematics is a standard level course intended for candidates who have high degree of competency in mathematics and intend to study mathematics at a higher level both beyond the IB program.

Unlike other courses, Further Mathematics is not intended to be taken on its own, but rather as an extension of the Mathematics HL course. While the course contains topics from the HL course, it is studied at the SL level.

Structure

The course is made up of 5 topics. While the first topic is unique, topics 2-5 are the option topics from Mathematics HL, all of which are covered.
1. Geometry
2. Statistics and probability
3. Sets, relations and groups
4. Series and differential equations
5. Discrete mathematics

Assessments

As Further Mathematics is taken in conjunction with Mathematics HL, there is no external assessment for the course.

There are two papers in the external assessment for Further Mathematics.

Paper 1 is worth 35% of the final mark. It is composed of four to six short-response questions which are based on the whole course. The paper lasts 1 hour.

Paper 2 is worth 65% of the final mark. It is composed of four to six extended-response questions which are based on the whole course. The paper lasts 2 hours.

Prior Knowledge

The prior knowledge is the same for Mathematics HL & SL as well as Further Mathematics.

Numbers and algebra

- Routine use of addition, subtraction, multiplication and division using integers, decimals and fractions; including order of operations.
- Simple positive exponents.
- Simplification of expressions involving roots (surds or radicals).
- Prime numbers and factors, including greatest common factors and least common multiples.
- Simple applications of ratio, percentage and proportion, linked to similarity.
- Definition and elementary treatment of absolute value (modulus).
- Rounding, decimal approximations and significant figures, including appreciation of errors.
- Expression of numbers in standard form (scientific notation)
- Concept and notation of sets, elements, universal (reference) set, empty (null) set, complement, subset, equality of sets, disjoint sets. Operations on sets: union and intersection.
- Commutative, associative and distributive properties.
- Venn diagrams.
- Number systems: natural numbers; integers, Z ; rationals, Q, and irrationals; real numbers, R.
- Intervals on the real number line using set notation and using inequalities. Expressing the solution set of a linear inequality on the number line and in set notation.
- The concept of a relation between the elements of one set and between the elements of one set and those of another set. Mappings of the elements of one set onto or into another, or the same, set.
- Illustration by means of tables, diagrams and graphs.
- Basic manipulation of simple algebraic expressions involving factorization and expansion.
- Rearrangement, evaluation and combination of simple formulae.
- The linear function $xax + b$ and its graph, gradient and y-

intercept.

- Addition and subtraction of algebraic fractions with denominators of the form $ax + b$.

- The properties of order relations: $<$, $\leq$, $>$, $\geq$.

- Solution of equations and inequalities in one variable including cases with rational coefficients.

- Solution of simultaneous equations in two variables.

Geometry

- Elementary geometry of the plane including the concepts of dimension for point, line, plane and space.

- Parallel and perpendicular lines, including $m1 = m2$, and $1\,2\,m$ $m = -1$. Geometry of simple plane figures.

- The function $xax + b$: its graph, gradient and y-intercept.

- Angle measurement in degrees. Compass directions and bearings. Right-angle trigonometry.

- Simple applications for solving triangles.

- Pythagorean' theorem and its converse.

- The Cartesian plane: ordered pairs (x, y) , origin, axes. Midpoint of a line segment and distance between two points in the Cartesian plane.

- Simple geometric transformations: translation, reflection, rotation, enlargement. Congruence and similarity, including the concept of scale factor of an enlargement.

- The circle, its centre and radius, area and circumference. The terms "arc", "sector", "chord", "tangent" and "segment".

- Perimeter and area of plane figures. Triangles and quadrilaterals, including parallelograms, rhombuses, rectangles, squares, kites and trapeziums (trapezoids); compound shapes.

Statistics

- Descriptive statistics: collection of raw data, display of data in pictorial and diagrammatic forms.

- Calculation of simple statistics from discrete data, including mean, median and mode.

Computer Science

IB Computer Science focuses on developing logical problem solving skills as well as educating candidates about computer systems.

The course works mainly with the Java programming language and candidates are expected to acquire a degree of mastery aspects of the language.

Computer Science guides candidates through learning by identifying and defining problems to be solved in a computerized system, breaking them into parts and constructing appropriate algorithms to create a solution.

There are four main objectives in IB Computer Science:

1. Demonstrate an understanding of: terminology, concepts, processes, structures, techniques, principles, systems and consequences (social significance and implications) of computing.
2. Apply and use: terminology, concepts, processes, structures, techniques, principles and systems of computing.
3. Analyze, discuss and evaluate: terminology, concepts, processes, structures, techniques, principles, systems and consequences (social significance and implications) of computing.
4. Construct: processes, structures, techniques and systems of computing.

Take note that IB Computer Science does not fulfill the requirements of group 5, though it may be taken in lieu of a group 6 subject to fulfill the requirements for that group.

Structure

Both HL and SL classes complete a core of three topics:
1. Systems life cycle and software development
2. Program construction in Java
3. Computing system fundamentals

HL classes study four additional topics at a deeper level:

4. Computer mathematics and logic
5. Abstract data structures and algorithms
6. Further system fundamentals
7. File organization

Additionally, both HL and SL classes study a case study which is constructed every two years by the IB. This case study accompanies the standard course work at both levels and familiarity with it is tested by one question during paper 2 of the external assessment.

Assessments

The internal assessment for IB Computer Science is worth 35% of the final mark for both HL and SL candidates. It consists of a program dossier which addresses and provides a solution to a single problem chosen by the candidate under advisement.

The analysis, design, and production of the final system must be well documented and is focused on constructing appropriate classes, implementing algorithms and data structures in Java.

The external assessment consists of two papers, each worth 32.5% of the final mark for HL and SL candidates.

Paper 1 has two sections:

A. This section consists of several short-answer questions which mainly test course objectives 1 and 2. For HL candidates, the questions are based on both the core and additional topics studied. For SL candidates, they are based only on the core topics

B. This section consists of six structured questions for HL candidates and four questions for SL candidates. The questions mainly test course objectives 3 and 4.

Paper 1 lasts 2.25 hours for HL candidates and 1.5 hours for SL candidates.

Paper 2 consists of several extended response questions in several parts.

- The first set of questions requires candidates to construct appropriate algorithms based on appropriate scenarios. HL candidates answer three questions while SL candidates answer two.

- The final question is structured in several parts and is based on the case study covered during the course. Both HL and SL classes complete this question.

Paper 2 lasts 2.25 hours for HL candidates and 1.5 hours for SL candidates.

Group 6
The Arts

Group 6 - The Arts is composed of six subjects that aim to enable candidates become engaged with the arts while being informed, reflective, and critical practitioners of the subjects they study.

Candidates are expected to express ideas with confidence and competence while developing their perceptual and analytical skills.

There are currently five courses in Group 6:
1. Dance
2. Music
3. Visual Arts
4. Theatre Arts
5. Film

The courses in Group 6 are considered optional electives. While candidates must complete at least one course from every other subject group, completion of a Group 6 course is not necessary to receive an IB diploma.

Completion of the computer science course from Group 5 can also fulfill the requirements for Group 6.

Dance

For 2011-2012, Dance is a new course available at both standard and higher levels. The curriculum of dance seeks to combine learning about culture, techniques, and styles in dance while developing performance skills. Prior experience is not required for SL courses, but is strongly recommended for HL courses.

Structure

IB Dance consists of three parts: composition and analysis, world dance studies, and performance.

Composition and analysis is an investigation into the creation of dances, the components of a dance as well as historical and cultural backgrounds. Candidates also compose two (SL) or three (HL) short original works during this section of the course.

World dance studies explores dancing traditions around the world in order to better understand dancing from both physical (artistic) and theoretical standpoints.

Performance involves practice and development of a candidate's dance skills. This section of the course allows candidates to hone the works that they have created in preparation for assessment.

Assessment

The internal assessment is a performance of one (SL) or two (HL) original dances that are chosen by the candidate from the works they have created during the course. Each performance lasts 3-6 (SL) or 6-9 (HL) minutes and a recorded copy is submitted to the IBO on DVD for evaluation.

The performance is worth 40% of the final mark.

Additionally, candidates write a formal report on the dances that they have created that focuses on comparing the differences and similarities between the two dances that they have created. The report is no more than 1,500 (SL) or 2,500 (HL) words and is worth 25% of the final mark.

The external assessment consists of all the dance works that a candidate has created which are recorded and submitted to the

IBO on a DVD. These performances do not need to be done formally with audience or costume. The total presentation is 6-10 (SL) or 8-15 (HL) minutes and is accompanied by an analytical statement of no more than 800 (SL) or 1,000 (HL) words that documents and reflects on one of the works created.

The external assessment is worth 60% of the final mark.

Music

IB Music aims to develop the knowledge and potential of candidates as musicians. The course teaches musical terminology, comparative analysis of music in relation to time, place, and culture, as well as creative and performance skills.

Structure

The course has several pathways. All levels study the core component: Musical Perception.

HL candidates also study components on Creating and Solo Performing.

SL candidates choose one of three options to study in addition to the core component:
1. Creating (SLC)
2. Solo Performing (SLS)
3. Group Performing (SLG)

Assessment

The internal assessment is worth 50% of the final mark for both HL and SL candidates. The options chosen in the course define the nature of the internal assessment. HL candidates complete Creating and Solo Performing while SL candidates choose one of the three options:

Creating consists of three pieces of coursework, with recordings and written work.

Solo Performing consists of a recording selected from pieces presented during one or more public performances.

Group Performing consists of a recording selected from pieces presented during two or more public performances.

The external assessment for Music is made up two papers.

Paper 1 is a listening paper and is worth 30% of the final mark for HL and SL candidates. The paper is made up of several questions which test musical perception and is given in three parts:

- Section A requires candidates answer two of three questions.

- Section B requires candidates to answer three of four questions.

- Section C is for HL candidates only and consists of one question.

Paper 2 is a musical links investigation. Candidates write a media script which investigates significant musical links between two (or more) pieces from distinct musical cultures.

Visual Arts

The course in Visual Arts focuses on enabling candidates to actively explore the arts through both artistic creation and investigation. Visual Arts offers candidates the opportunity to build on prior artistic experience while developing new skills, techniques and ideas.

Candidates are expected not only to develop their personal artistic skills, but also to explore and critically analyze qualities of past, present, and emerging arts.

For IB Visual Arts, there is very little difference between HL and SL courses.

While the structure is the same at both levels of the course, HL candidates have a much larger volume of time in which to create not only a larger body of work, but also work with greater depth.

Structure

The content of the course is fundamentally split between 60 % studio work and 40% learning through the creation investigation workbooks which are composed of both visual and written investigation.

This division is fundamental though the course strives to maintain an integrated relationship between studio work and investigation work.

Investigation workbooks are integral to the course and reflect the candidate's visual and written investigation.

Additionally, HL and SL candidates must choose to pursue one of two options in their course work.

Option A is for candidates who wish to concentrate on refining their studio work. Candidates produce their investigative workbooks to support, inform, develop, and refine their studio work.

Option B takes the opposite approach of Option A. Candidates in Option B create workbooks which fully explore a range of ideas within a contextual, visual and critical framework. They then produce studio work based on their visual and written investigation.

Assessments

The internal and external assessments for Visual Arts are composed of the studio and investigative work.

The studio assessment is composed of an exhibition made up of the selected studio work of the candidate.

The assessment into the investigation workbooks consists of the candidate presenting selected pages of his or her investigation workbooks which have been composed during the course.

If the candidate has pursued the Option A:

The studio work is considered as the external assessment. The work is evaluated by a visiting examiner following an interview with each candidate. The external assessment is worth 60% of the final mark.

The investigative workbook is considered as the internal assessment and is evaluated by the teacher. The internal assessment is worth 40% of the final mark.

If the candidate has pursued Option B:

The investigative workbook is considered as the external assessment. The work is evaluated by a visiting examiner following an interview with the candidate.

The external assessment is worth 60% of the final mark.

The studio work is considered as the internal assessment and is evaluated by the teacher.

The internal assessment is worth 40% of the final mark.

Theatre Arts

IB Theatre Arts is a course which aims to familiarize and encourage development of candidates' expressional abilities through their organizational and technical skills in theatre. The course strives to not only enrich candidates' knowledge of theatre but to also increase their skills in theatre and increase awareness in understanding the creative expression of others.

Like the course in Visual Arts, there is not much structural difference between the course at HL and SL levels. While the work produced may not differ significantly, HL candidates are expected to use the extra time available to them to develop their personal knowledge and skills at a level beyond that of SL candidates.

Structure

The structure of IB Theatre Arts is not given as a strict syllabus, but rather as a flexible template which allows teachers to develop a syllabus unique to their program. As such, every theatre program will be individual and unique.

There are three core learning components to the course:

1. **Theatre in the Making**

   This section of the course is exploratory and deals with learning the process of making theatre rather than presenting theatre.

2. **Theatre in Performance**

   The second section of the course focuses on the application of skills developed in theatre in the making. This section sees candidates in various roles practicing the art of presenting theatre.

3. **Theatre in the World**

   The final section of the course focuses on a practical and theoretical exploration of a range of theatre traditions and practices from around the world.

In addition, candidates at both HL and SL levels are expected to keep a journal charting all aspects of their learning throughout the course. The journal can take whatever form the candidate wishes it to and reflects on their progress in learning theatre.

The final component to the course is the independent project. This project allows an independent exploration in theatre which is backed by a theoretical research into performance. It may be individually completed or involve other candidates in the class.

HL candidates have a choice of two options for their project.

Option A focuses on candidates assuming the role of a director/creator in order to explore the process of devising and creating a performance.

Option B focuses on exploring aspects of theatre practices and involves candidates either examine the theories or work of one or more theatre forms or demonstrating and understanding of theatre technique through performance.

SL candidates present a project which increases the candidates' knowledge and skills in a specific area of theatre. To accomplish this, candidates create and present an original piece of work inspired by any source of the candidate's choice.

Assessments

The assessment structure is identical for both HL and SL candidates.

The internal assessment is worth 50% of the final mark and consists of two equally weighted parts:

- The first part is a theatre performance and an oral production presentation.

  The presentation lasts 30 minutes for HL and 20 minutes for SL candidates

- The second part of the assessment consists of a portfolio about the independent project and its connection to their experiences in the core subjects of the course.

The external assessment is worth 50% of the final mark and consists of two equally weighted parts:

- The first part consists of a research investigation with supporting visual materials

- The second part consists of a practical performance proposal with supporting visual materials.

HL candidates also complete a written report in conjunction with the proposal.

Film

The objective of IB Film is to develop candidates' skills so that they are adept at both interpreting and making film texts. The course explores film history, theory, and socioeconomic background, developing the critical abilities of candidates in their appreciation of film.

As well, the course emphasizes development of professional and technical skills in film creation.

Structure

The course consists of three main parts for all candidates:

1. Textual Analysis: Both HL and SL candidates are required to study one extract from a film and offer a detailed analysis of the extract within the context of the film as a whole.

2. Film theory and history: HL candidates study at least four films from more than one country while SL candidates study two.

3. Creative Process: both HL and SL candidates create and produce an original film as part of a team or as an individual. HL candidates also create an individual trailer for the film production.

Assessments

The assessment structure is similar for both HL and SL candidates.

The internal assessment is worth 50% of the final mark and consists of a completed original film project with accompanying written documentation. While the project may be completed as a group, this documentation must be produced individually.

The external assessment is worth 50% of the final mark and consists of two equally weighted parts:

1. Independent study where a candidate produces a rationale, script, and list of sources for a short documentary production on an aspect of film theory or film history

This is based on a study of at least four films for HL candidates and two films for SL candidates.

2. An oral presentation of a detailed critical analysis of a continuous extract from a prescribed film.

Other Courses

Beyond the standard courses, the IB offers some specialty courses. These classes are available on a limited basis. If you have the opportunity to take one, it can be an interesting diversion from the normal IB curriculum.

Piloted Courses

Piloted subjects are courses that the IB is currently developing and testing. Some of these courses will go on to become standardized parts of the IB curriculum. For 2011-2012, the majority of piloted courses (Dance, World Religions, Literature & Performance) have been introduced as normal courses.

School Based Courses

School based courses are curriculums developed independently by teachers at an individual school along with the guidance and approval from the IB.

A school-based course may only replace courses in groups 2 or 6 only and every course is taught at the standard level.

Online Courses

The IB is currently developing a pilot version of the diploma version so that any candidate around the world may study in the IB program.

Experienced IB teachers will teach courses online in a virtual classroom. This allows candidates who do not have access to an IB school to take IB courses as well as allowing candidates the opportunity to take IB courses their school may not offer.

Currently, the program offers a limited number of courses and is continuously being expanded with new courses. For more information, ask your coordinator or check out:

www.ibo.org/diploma/development/dponline

http://www.pamojaeducation.com/

Other Courses

4   ***Core Elements***

Beyond the six subject groups, there are three core elements of the IB program which all diploma candidates must complete in order to matriculate.

These are the Theory of Knowledge course (TOK), the Extended Essay research project (EE), and Creativity Action Service hours (CAS).

This section provides a deeper guide to each of these three components, what they require, and advice for doing well in each one.

Theory of Knowledge

Theory of Knowledge is a course that is required for all diploma candidates. The objective of TOK is to guide students into a better understanding of what knowledge is and how they come to know.

Many students are misled into thinking that TOK is a course in philosophy. TOK is distinctly different than philosophy as it deals with how knowledge exists and how we are able to know something rather than the discussion of already existent knowledge and thought.

The core of TOK is based around one question: How do you know? In the TOK course, this "knowing" is interpreted to be a "justified true belief".

Thusly, much of the coursework concerns discussion and investigation of what "true belief" actually is and then attempting to justify it through supported, rational argument.

To do this, students first interpret the "four ways of knowing": sensual perception, emotion, reason, and language.

These "ways of knowing" are then applied to the seven "areas of knowledge":

1. Mathematics
2. Natural Sciences
3. Social Sciences
4. History
5. The Arts
6. Ethics
7. Spirituality

Note that these are very close to the six core subject areas of the diploma program.

Finally, students are asked questions that directly relate to their everyday acquisition of knowledge. Some examples of these include:

How do you know that the scientific method is a valid method of gaining knowledge?

What is the reason for having historical knowledge, and how is it applied in life?

In this way, the course pushes students to examine the learning process on a deeper level and subsequently reexamine their learning throughout the entire diploma program.

Assessment

Unlike the other subject groups in the diploma program, TOK does not have a cumulative exam. Instead, students give an internal assessment that consists of a ten-minute oral presentation on a topic of the student's choice.

Additionally there is a final essay of about 1,200-1,600 words which is written on one of 10 pre-determined questions which are changed every year.

In both the presentation and essay, students are evaluated on their used of the knowledge assessment ideas and techniques discussed in the course. Using these techniques and ideas to support and defend your argument is essential to a good final score in Theory of Knowledge.

It is important to note that a passing grade in TOK is necessary to receive your diploma. Most students find that simply attending class and giving a relatively concerted effort towards in-class discussion, the oral presentation and the essay gets them a good grade.

TOK is a qualitative course and unlike more traditional subjects does not lend itself to a strict quantitative grading scheme.

Keep in mind however that a good score in TOK can give you up to three extra points in your final score towards your diploma.

The Extended Essay

The Extended Essay (EE) is an integral and unique part of the IB program. As a core component, it is a task that all candidates must complete successfully in order to receive an IB diploma.

What it is

The Extended Essay is a formal research paper that is devised, conducted, and written by the student. While similar to a senior project, it is expected to be more complex and demanding and in many ways is similar to the thesis papers that students in Switzerland and other countries write at the end of their high school education.

During the course of an Extended Essay, candidates conduct extensive research and study into the topic of their choosing from one of the six IB subject groups. This allows candidates to show knowledge and understanding, not only in a specific subject, but also in the skills that are necessary to complete the project.

The Extended Essay is a synthesis of the skills that you are expected to acquire during the IB program. Specifically, these are critical inquiry and analysis, engagement in systematic research and learning, as well as developing research and presentation skills.

Timing and other considerations

While the Extended Essay is independent from any class, the time demands of the project are equal to that of any other course. Successful candidates are expected to spend at least 40 hours on the Extended Essay, so it is essential to build time for it into your daily schedule. The biggest challenge students face when writing the Extended Essay is not starting to work on it early enough and waiting to complete critical sections of the project until the last possible moment.

This is an essential project so it is imperative to set aside enough time to complete it. As well, the Extended Essay usually takes longer to finish than you think it will. My Extended Essay project morphed itself from a simple interview to a full blown oral history project. My problem was not figuring out what to write, but what to take out.

While the exact schedule will vary from school to school, the Extended Essay process generally begins around February during the first year of the IB program. During February/March, you will select a topic and develop a formal research proposal. You will also either be assigned, or request a faculty advisor to assist you in the project.

Following these initial steps, you will begin your research, and over the summer , as well as into the next school year you will write the Extended Essay.

Ideally, you will finish a final draft sometime between December and February of your senior year.

The biggest hurdle that students face in this timeline is summer break. Many (if not most) people do little or nothing over the summer. When fall comes, not only is there a lot of work to be done on the Extended Essay, but there is also the senior year IB workload, PLUS college applications, essays, etc. I definitely procrastinated a little more than I should have and spent many long, caffeine induced nights transcribing, researching, and writing. Avoid this at all costs.

During the summer, things can be more flexible. This is prime time to get *a lot* done on your Extended Essay. The essay does not have to be finished by the start of school in the fall; however, a draft will take you a long way in getting a better grade on the final product and making senior year much less stressful. In a nutshell: you're going to have a lot on your plate, so start early.

Choosing a topic

Choosing a subject and topic is perhaps the most important step in writing the Extended Essay. Picking a topic without considering the final outcome of your project can have serious consequences several months down the line. On the other hand, changing topics mid-way through is very doable, and although I do not advise it, I know several successful IB candidates who changed their topics a month, or even weeks before the final deadline.

The best advice is to pick a topic in which you have a genuine interest. Do not pick a topic simply because it "has candor" or seems impressive.

Try to avoid choosing a topic that is obviously over everyone's head (including yours). Without comprehensible sources you will end up frustrated and regretting your choice in topic while writing an Extended Essay that is complete gibberish.

Rather than trying too hard and hating yourself in the process, the path to a good Extended Essay is through a subject and topic that motivate you. Find something that will drive you even when the nights are long and the days are dark; a topic that you love and that will keep you interested for a year of research and writing.

Start with something you are familiar with - and good at. If you are great at biology and growing plants, maybe consider something that has to do with plant genetics and breeding. Your essay will just be a big lab project. On the other hand, if you are love reading and literature evaluation, consider doing a critical evaluation of one, or even several books.

Try to choose a manageable topic. Pick something that has substance, but at the same time can be focused and specific. Getting into too small of a niche can have its drawbacks, however biting off more than you can chew often proves to be very dangerous.

You may find that your initial topic, although focused, is still too broad to really get a good grasp on. This can be good to start, however, narrowing a topic down and eventually focusing on a single question or aspect is beneficial to your grade and the amount of work that you do.

The Extended Essay is a chance to learn more about what you like to do and to tell other people about it. If you are passionate about your topic, it can easily become one of the most enjoyable parts of the IB diploma program.

The Importance of your Advisor

To properly navigate your subject, you are required to have a faculty adviser. An adviser is the main source of help that students receive when developing the Extended Essay. Your adviser must be a teacher at your school and in some way be related to the topic which you are studying. My Extended Essay was an oral history project, so my advisor was my history teacher and IB coordinator, Mr. Guy Thomas.

A good advisor will help you to understand your subject, as well as make sure that your research, paper, and presentation all conform to the standards set by the IB. The advisor should also spend time looking over your first draft (they are not allowed to edit), as well as help you to find the resources that you need to successfully complete your project.

Advisors take their role very seriously and the evaluation of your Extended Essay is augmented by a report that is written by your advisor. You will also spend a lot of time with them, so its a good idea to find someone who you like. Not getting along with your advisor can make the Extended Essay into a miserable experience, even if you have a good topic.

How it works

The Extended Essay is a formal research paper and it has certain specifications to how it should be presented. While you certainly can alter the order, it is important to include these sections in order to receive the best possible grade

Title:

This should make the focus of the essay very clear. It should be precise and not drawn-out or long-winded.

Abstract:

The abstract presents an overview of the essay. It is not an introduction, but rather a synthesis. For this reason, it is best to write the abstract last. The abstract is limited to 300 words. The abstract should cover
- The research question being investigated

- The scope of the investigation
- The conclusion(s) of the Extended Essay.

The abstract should be typed or word processed on one side of a sheet of paper, and placed immediately after the title page.

Contents Page:

The contents page is placed at the beginning of the essay and lists the contents of the document. All pages must be numbered.

Body:

The main text of the Extended Essay is limited to 4,000 words or less. This word count only includes this main text, not the abstract, contents, or any illustrations.

Surpassing these limits can bring on penalties as IB examiners are not required to read more than 4,000 words of your paper. At the same time, you should probably write at least 2,000 words in order for your essay to be taken seriously.

Illustrations:

Extended essays are expected to be organized and neat. While they are not required, illustrations can go a long way in presenting your argument.

If you use graphs, tables, or photographs: be sure to cite their original sources and explain their purpose if necessary. Any illustrations should directly relate to the text where they are located. Like bad writing, if an illustration does not add to your essay, you should probably not include it.

Bibliographies, references, citations:

As part of academic and intellectual honesty, the Extended Essay should precisely and accurately reference any quotations, ideas, or points of view. A bibliography comes after your paper and is an exact list of all of the sources which you have used and cited in the Extended Essay.

Be sure to properly format your bibliography in an accepted major style that is appropriate for your sources.

Appendices, footnotes, end notes:

These sections are not required for the Extended Essay and it is best to avoid lengthy appendices and end notes if possible.

Constantly referring to the appendix during the essay interrupts the continuity and fluidity of the work. As well, having large written appendices can be seen as an attempt to evade the word limit and may carry severe penalty.

Include what is necessary, but do not rely on an appendix to support your essay.

The research

The research you do is a crucial part to the Extended Essay. Through trial, error, and constant refinement, I have found that there are essentially seven steps to getting your research off the ground:

1. Choose an approved IB subject area for the essay. Ask your advisor or consult the official Extended Essay guide if you are having doubts.

2. Choose a topic that motivates you.

3. Create a focused, direct research question. Narrow down your topic and find a specific question that intrigues you.

4. Plan the investigation and the writing process. Layout how you are going to research the material that you need as well and set deadlines for each step of your plan.

5. Write an outline. Plan the structure of your essay. This will help you focus your research and will give you a sense of direction from the onset.

6. Do some initial reading. Conduct some Google searches and visit your local library. Read up on your topic to get a feel for what the research will entail.

   If you cannot find enough information, you may want to consider changing your topic. At the very least, talk to your advisor. You might just need to refocus in order to find more information and expand on your original topic.

7. Start researching. Your research should be planned and methodological. Keep records of what you read and where you find it.

One of the biggest problems students have when writing the Extended Essay is where to find good information.

On the Internet, I always start with Google searches and Wikipedia. While you cannot cite Wikipedia directly, often times the list of sources for articles proves to be invaluable. As well, Google has some great tools for searching through published academic papers. Other good research sites include JSTOR, Infomine, and Gale. See "links" in the appendix.

Offline, one of the best places to find specialized material is a university library. If you have a university nearby, go and find what you need. Make photocopies and only check out what you need to. As well, many university libraries have correspondence programs where they will mail you materials that you need. Check the library website for details.

If you want more information on conducting research, check out "Research like a Pro" in chapter 8.

The Viva Voce

The viva voce is a very important part of your Extended Essay project. Viva voce is Latin for "live voice" and essentially, this is a presentation and interview with your advisor about your Extended Essay.

Do not be intimidated by the viva voce, it is an opportunity for you to shed light on your work and to explain what you have done. The viva voce is a central part of the advisor's report to the IB. It helps your advisor and the IB to better understand what you have done.

Additionally, the viva voce serves as a vetting session that gives you an opportunity to reflect on what you have learned and accomplished during the Extended Essay.

Part of the grading for the Extended Essay allows your adviser to note particular persistence in the face of difficulty and intellectual inventiveness - this is the time to show off how much you have accomplished.

The viva voce is essentially a short interview with your advisor and should not take more than 10-15 minutes. Do not stress, it is not an interrogation but rather an opportunity to show just how much you have learned about your topic.

Getting better marks (what to do)

While all this regulation may seem overwhelming and strict, there are many things you can do to boost your final grade for the Extended Essay.

Have a point: you need to have a clear and developed thesis statement. Every part of your essay should be laid out as to support your thesis statement. Refer back to it when necessary and do not write anything that does not have a clear reason for being in your essay.

Get real about your grade: The Extended Essay is graded on an A-E scale. Receiving an A on your Extended Essay is extremely difficult to do, though that being said, receiving a C or above for your Extended Essay is not something to be worried about and in fact means that you did a good job.

While you *can* receive an E on the Extended Essay and still get your diploma, this is at best a dangerous scenario. If you score an E for both the Extended Essay and TOK, you will not receive an IB diploma. For information on passing scores, see the scoring worksheet in the appendix.

What not to do

The one thing you do not want to do in the Extended Essay is plagiarize. Your work and your ideas should be your own. If not all of your words are yours, make sure to say so and make it clear. If you are not certain what plagiarism is, read up on academic honesty in chapter 9.

Again, do not pick a topic that you are going to end up hating. If you end up with a topic that you find repulsive or boring, consider an immediate switch to something more stimulating.

Do not wait until the last minute. Start as soon as possible.

Finally, do not stress. Four thousand words is actually very little after all of the research you will do. Most people are forced to edit their original drafts down from 8,000 or even 10,000 words to get what they want to say to fit in 4,000.

It is important to work hard on the Extended Essay, however do not sacrifice *all* of your time in order to put out a marginally better paper. IB evaluators know that you already have a lot going on with homework, test preparation, and applying to college.

The IB is not looking for a revolutionary study or ground-breaking research in an Extended Essay, only that you have the ability to organize and communicate ideas fluidly and that you can apply what you have learned in the diploma program to complete a large project.

CAS

CAS stands for Creativity, Action, and Service. The CAS program is essentially time which is spent outside of the classroom doing rather than thinking. This program is an important core component of the IB diploma.

In keeping with the IB ethos of a worldly and rounded academic program, CAS forces students to expand beyond academics and provides a counterbalance to the academic rigors of the IB program.

CAS is founded on the principle of "Think globally, act locally" as well as the concept that in order for learning, speaking, and writing to be effective, there must be action taken from what is learned.

Completing CAS successfully is absolutely necessary in order to receive an IB diploma.

Components of CAS

There are three types of CAS hours:

1. Creativity:

   Time spent with the arts or any other experience that involves creative thinking

2. Action:

   Any activity involving physical movement, exercise or sport that compliments other work done in the diploma program.

3. Service:

   Time spent helping others in a voluntary or unpaid position.

In the time spent doing CAS, students are expected to achieve eight learning outcomes in each area. These outcomes are not rated or graded; rather students should ask themselves, "Have I achieved this?":

1. Increased awareness for personal strengths and areas for growth
2. Undertaken new challenges
3. Planned and initiated activities
4. Worked collaboratively with others
5. Shown perseverance and commitment in activities
6. Engaged with issues of global importance
7. Considered the ethical implications of actions
8. Developed new skills

Requirements and Reflection

Any activities that are logged as CAS must be real, purposeful, and have a significant outcome. CAS hours often provide a personal challenge and it is expected that you give your CAS time significant thought and consideration. This includes time spent to plan, review, and report your CAS activities as well as a reflection on the outcomes of the activities and what you learned.

This may sound a bit fluffly, so remember to not take CAS **too** seriously. CAS is a time to have fun, do something outside and give back a bit to yourself and people around you. I approached CAS as school required fun. Find enjoyable tasks for CAS and this becomes an easy, enjoyable part of the diploma program.

For my CAS hours, I donated to and volunteered at several charity auctions, played in my high school marching band, and did volunteer work for several local parks.

While CAS hours are not formally assessed, it is expected that students document their CAS activities and provide evidence that they have achieved the eight learning outcomes for each of the three CAS areas. While some learning outcomes may be repeated many times during a CAS activity, and others very little it is only important to show that there is **some** evidence of having achieved every outcome.

The student reflection is one of the most important parts of the CAS program as it proves to the IB that you have fulfilled the necessary requirements for CAS.

This reflection can take on many different forms including blogs, journals, video or visual display. Detail of the activities should be included; however, extensive documentation of routine experiences is not necessary.

Some of the best reporting comes when there is a real audience and purpose to the documentation such as informing a community about plans or programs.

To ensure successful completion of the CAS requirements, students will meet with their CAS advisor at least twice during the first year and once during the second. This ensures that the student is on track to matriculate.

In the past, completion of CAS mandated that a specific number of recorded hours were fulfilled. While the program has been revised so that there are no specific hourly requirements, the IB recommends spending about 3 hours a week doing CAS activities.

Activities

The options for CAS activities are many and varied. Creating music with a band or playing on a sporting team are respectively two great examples of creativity and action activities. Service activities must provide real, tangible learning benefits for the students.

In general, any activity that is mundane or completed without thought and refection does not count for CAS. Time spent in CAS should be considered carefully so that it benefits the student in some way.

Undertaking meaningless activity simply for the sake of CAS does not fulfill the goals or requirements of the program.

There are a few activities for which counting, as CAS can be negotiable. In general, the touchiest areas include political and religious activity. While there are many types of these activities that can be counted as CAS, some such as religious proselytizing and political activity which causes or worsen social division are not appropriate.

In the case that some of your CAS activities involve politics or religion, it is best to use discretion, good judgment, and consultation with your CAS adviser or Diploma program coordinator.

Beyond this, the sky is the limit and any number of activities that you already do may be considered for CAS hours pending they incorporate learning and reflection.

The goal of CAS is not for students to mindlessly do extracurricular activities, but rather to engage in the world around them and begin to learn beyond the classroom.

Survival

Run when you can, walk when you have
to, crawl if you must:
just never give up

-Dean Karnazes

5 ***Diploma Survival***

Since every course grade in the IB is based off of examination, the internal and external assessments are the most crucial parts of the diploma program. You do not earn an IB diploma by attendance, so receiving good marks for your work done in the assessments is very important.

That being the case, the IB assessments often leave students confused and stressed. Like much of the IB program, figuring out exactly how they work can be a baffling process. Undoubtedly, there are a lot of regulations and requirements; however, things are not as complicated as they might seem at first.

Each IB examination is based around a common core structure, understanding this structure makes preparing and sitting for exams much simpler and less stressful.

There are two types of examinations in IB: the internal and external assessments. Every course in the diploma program includes both types.

For most courses, the internal assessment is weighted less than the external assessment. Usually, the internal assessment is worth 20-30 percent of the final grade, while the external assessment is worth 70-80 percent of the final grade.

Internal Assessments

The internal assessment is the component of the IB examinations that takes place during the course. The internal assessment takes the form of a major project, or portfolio collection based on work that is done during the course.

The exact form of an internal assessment is unique to each course.

For science or art courses, the internal assessment will usually take the form of a collection of work done by the student during the course.

For humanities and language courses, the internal assessment will often be a project accompanied by some type of oral evaluation.

For the course in psychology, the internal assessment is an experiment that is created and carried out by students.

Grading

Unlike a normal examination, the internal assessment is graded by the course instructor who evaluates the work according to requirements set up by the IB. After the assessments for the course are graded, the instructor will send their grades, along with several samples of the work from the class to the IB.

Trained and impartial evaluators will then re-grade the sample work and adjust the scores for the entire class accordingly. This means that while the course instructor grades internal assessments, the IB moderates this grading so that any errors or bias in an instructor's grading can be adjusted for.

Tips

Scoring high marks on an internal assessment can be deceptively difficult. Unlike most American schools, the IB evaluates based on the assumption that the majority of students receive a 'C'. Getting an 'A' grade is difficult and means that you have done truly significant work.

Do not blow off your internal assessment. It may not be a timed examination, but it is a crucial part to receiving high marks in your IB courses. Put the same effort into your internal assessment that you would put into a final IB exam.

Spend as much time as necessary to complete the assessment to the best of your ability. Study for you assessment and do not wait until the last minute to complete what you need to do.

If you can, get the mark scheme that your work will be graded against and use it as a guide when you create your internal assessment. Ask someone to look over your project with the mark scheme and tell you how well he or she would rate you based on the requirements.

This allows you to tailor your work to the requirements for the assessment. If you can submit your assessment with the certainty that you have designed it to fulfill each requirement in the mark scheme to the best of your ability, you will undoubtedly score high marks.

How you do in your internal assessment does not necessarily mean that you will pass or fail the entire course. Still the internal assessment is worth anywhere from 20-50 percent of your grade, so its important. Use it as an opportunity to score points away from the pressures of the exam room.

External Assessments

The external assessments, also known as the IB examinations, are the final tests of what you have learned in each IB course. For most courses, the majority of the grade is based off of the external assessment.

For the majority of schools in the northern hemisphere, all IB exams take place in May, schools in the southern hemisphere test in November. You will only take an IB exam at the end of a course. This means that you will not take the final examination for a two-year HL course until the end of your second year in the course.

External examinations are taken at your school in a tightly controlled environment. Usually the IB coordinator at the school is in charge of running the examinations; though in larger schools a specially trained "invigilator" from the school's faculty may be appointed to administer the exams.

Content

Each course examination consists of one to three separate papers which are taken at different times and usually on different days. An exam for a single course may take place over one or two weeks, while the entire exam season lasts around 4 weeks.

An examination paper can last from 45 minutes up to two hours. As well, due to the amount of papers that diploma candidates complete during the examination season, you may find yourself sitting for up to three papers in a single day. This is especially true for second year students sitting for HL examinations

Each examination paper is usually made up of only one or two different types of questions. Overall, you can expect to see seven different types of standard questions

1. essays
2. structured problems
3. short-response questions
4. data-response questions

5. text-response questions
6. case-study questions
7. multiple-choice questions

Grading

External assessments are evaluated by a staff of approximately 5,000 trained IB examiners who are located around the globe. The assessments are scored according to a carefully moderated set of criteria. Each paper is graded individually and counts for a certain percentage of your final grade.

This means that while the external assessment for a course may be worth 80% of the final grade: paper 1 may be worth 50% of the final grade while paper 2 is worth 30% of the final grade.

Obviously, some examination papers are more important than others are. Papers with higher weighting in a course's assessment will be longer, more complex, and more difficult.

Tips

Taking the IB exams is without any doubt the most overwhelming and stressful part of the IB experience. This is the make or break moment where all of your preparation and effort during your courses becomes obvious.

If you have put in the preparation, the examination season will be doable and bearable. If not, you may find yourself in a caffeine-induced stasis cramming night and day in order to prepare.

To cut down on the overload from stress, lack of sleep and non-stop studying for weeks on end, it is important to anticipate the exam season.

Start your preparation early. Try to study every week like you are preparing for the exams; do not wait until the last possible moment to really hit the books. Participate in mock exams as often as possible. If there are not enough opportunities, test yourself at home as if you are taking the test at school.

If you come into the exam season at full speed, the shock of having to perform and remember everything all at once will be much less.

Beyond preparation, take care of yourself. Past a certain point, your brain stops remembering anything. Instead of cramming all night before you test in the morning, review what you think is most essential, get a good night's sleep and wake up early.

Always remember to eat breakfast before you sit for your exams as well as a solid lunch and dinner the day before. A lot of candidates will bring water bottles and snacks into the exams with them. I highly recommend bringing something to keep you going, especially if you are sitting for a long paper.

Caffeine can be great, but use it in moderation. Too much caffeine will make it extremely difficult to concentrate and will make you dehydrated which can seriously affect how well you can study and remember information during a test.

Dehydration can also cause huge headaches, which are extremely distracting, so it is important to drink a lot of water. Sports drinks are a good alternative; though try to avoid ones with too much sugar. Having a sugar crash in the middle of a test is not going to help your score.

When you finally sit to take your exams, relax. You have studied hard to get to this point. Take time to go over your answers and your essays and do not stress yourself out further by thinking about all the ways you can fail.

Instead, remind yourself that you know this stuff; you have been reading it, listening to it, writing about it, and learning it for months. Go into your exams with ease and confidence, you have what it takes, the IB exams are yours to conquer.

6   ***"Creative" Writing***

What to say when you do not know what to say.

Also known as hogwash, bunk, and BS; this is a delicate and special art. There will be times (if you haven't had them yet, believe me, there will be times) when you have to say something - but you do not know exactly what to say.

There will also come times where life gets in the way. Things come up, you get off schedule, and a lot has to be done, quickly. If you need to hack out a paper in less than ideal time - it's time to bring out the big guns of B.S.

When it comes down to the line, the ability to write something about nothing is to feign knowledge or interest in a topic, while really possessing little of either. Doing this successfully is one part improvisation, one-part sales, and one part documentation.

A well fluffed speech or essay gives off the charm, evidence, and conviction of a carefully executed presentation but takes much less time to construct and inevitably contains much less actual content while still conveying the main message. Some might mistake this with lying, however it is not.

Essentially, what you are creating is filler, words which lead the audience to believe that you know a great deal more about a subject than you actually do.

Ultimately, the main goal is to produce the required amount of content with as little thought and in as little time as necessary.

The Basics

To start, clear your mind. Over-thinking, planning, and careful analysis tend to cloud the mind and interrupt the natural thought stream that you are going to rely on to provide you with your most valuable material.

The next step is to start moving, just simply and not too quickly.

If you are writing a paper, begin by writing down exactly what it is you are supposed to be writing about. Restate the question you are trying to answer or the thesis you intend to prove.

If you are speaking, start with an introduction to your topic, describing the premise and any main ideas. Truthfully, the easiest parts of your speech or paper are going to be the beginning and end. Generalize and present any information that you know.

The key is not so much in WHAT you say, but HOW you present it. Start from the territory that you know, and then branch out.

Take these opening statements from Johnny and Suzie's essays. They are both writing about how the theme of loneliness pervades in the book "Of Mice and Men". Who's essay is better?

Johnny:

> The theme of loneliness features throughout many scenes in Of Mice and Men; it is often the dominant theme of sections during this story. This theme occurs during many circumstances throughout the book and is the driving force behind the development of many of the characters.

Suzie:

> Loneliness is a very important theme in Of Mice and Men. This theme is so central to the story that it is a major driving force behind the character development.

You can see that while both Johnny and Suzie have said the same thing. The difference is that Johnny took about twice as much space to say it. Johnny wins the B.S. prize here. Utilizing repetitive and detailed description of his main ideas, he can get more paper written than Suzie (though he may not score as high)

While his work is bound to be less concise, it will be the same required length as Suzie's and will take him less than half of the time to write.

Don't Reinvent the Wheel

After you have a good start and your mind is buzzing, it's time to actually get the thing done...and FAST. If you have 5000 words to write, this is no time to reinvent the wheel. There are many good essays, speeches, and ideas already out there for you to use. I like to think of this element as 'creative plagiarism'.

You are not going to be ripping of somebody else's paper or speech exactly as they wrote it – that is cheating. Turning in someone else's hard work as your own will not go over well in IB, see the academic honesty section for more details. However, there is no copyright on the basic ideas or the structure of a paper. As long as you restate things in your own words and viewpoint, no harm should come to you.

As a further note, use this with caution and good judgment. Look to others work for inspiration, just do not copy what they have said, especially other students papers. If you are unsure what constitutes plagiarism, take a look at chapter 9.

The best way to start a paper is using sources that already exist. Depending on your topic, there are different places to look. Wikipedia is great for history or scientific topics, spark notes has many good ideas for literary criticism.

My personal strategy is to do a Google search on the topic that I want to write about, read a few of the most relevant articles which pop up and then restate them into my own words with some personal flair. In fact, that's exactly how I wrote this chapter.

As you get what you want to say in your head, let it flow out. When you are writing, don't worry too much about exactly what you're saying, the word order, or spelling. All of that can come later. The most important thing is to let your ideas flow onto the page. Trust me on this one.

Editing down a paper is a lot easier than getting your ideas down. The same goes for a speech or presentation. Just let all the information that you know about the topic flow out of you. As you go, your nervousness will disappear and be replaced with an almost magical flow of energy. Your ideas may flow faster than you can write. If this starts, don't try to stop it. Take quick notes and keep going.

As your thoughts come out, be very descriptive. For example, instead of saying "The brown bear crossed over the mountain.", Try "The great big brown bear came lolloping over the mountain, his fur glistening in the sunlight and his eyes shining as he moved quickly down through the valley".

Adding in extra description not only gives some extra flair, it will instantly make your paper or presentation longer, give you extra time to think, and make things more interesting for your audience. Describe the hell out of things.

A good guide for any paper or presentation is to start with a generalized introduction, move on to a body and include three angles to your topic. These could be three arguments about your topic, three comparisons to other topics, or even three sub-topics that you have more to say on.

To finish it up, restate your introduction and briefly draw some simple, descriptive conclusions from your body. Spend a few minutes on a few good ending sentences, and **BAM** you have a paper written in half the time.

You can also use the techniques of over-analysis and descriptive padding from simple ideas in any on the spot scenarios. Like an impossibly hard question asked in class or practicing for an oral assessment.

Conviction

The last key to doing well at this is to be believable. Include as much supporting detail in your arguments as possible. In a paper or presentation, use tables, charts, and figures.

When speaking, base your argument off a starting fact and bring in other facts that corroborate it. Finally, have conviction. If you present your ideas with enough confidence and enthusiasm, they will be much more believable and interesting.

Cut out words like "Um" and "stuff" and highlight your conclusions with words phrases such as: "At the end of the day..." and "In conclusion..."

When to Use It

This is not going to win you any awards. Bullshitting is best reserved for do-or-die times only. The times when turning in something is better than nothing at all.

If you are extremely well organized, meticulous, focused, and nothing bad ever happens, you might just be lucky enough to get through IB without having to B.S. anything.

For everyone else, this is that secret weapon that you keep in your back pocket to use when all else fails. Use it sparingly and wisely. When the time comes, you will know it. Otherwise, if you feel comfortable answering a question or writing a paper without ripping off ideas or writing meaningless sentences, I suggest not adding too much fluff to your assignments.

Remember that while it may seem like B.S. to, you are actually tapping into your true creativity. The best B.S. is not bunk at all, but just that amazing feeling when you remember everything that you want to say, and relax enough to let your mind say it.

Writing fluff is a good way to get your creative mind working, especially when faced with insurmountable writer's block. As well, there are times when a good B.S. is the perfect basis for an amazing paper.

In short, try to avoid using these techniques on a regular basis; though if used with care and thought, they can prove to be a powerful tool in boosting your grade.

7   ***Staying Low Stress***

Its Sunday night, your extended essay needs final editing and is due on Wednesday. Your first choice college essay is half written and due in 6 hours, and to top it all off, you have two quizzes: chemistry and psychology the next morning.

In the IB Diploma program, expectations increase. Tardiness, late homework, and laziness are no longer allowed. Teachers expect a lot more from students than before, as do your parents and friends. Things get hectic pretty quickly.

Keeping the stress that comes alongside the IB program will help you to not only get better marks, but to retain your sanity.

Many people in our modern life are way too stressed out. Stress relating to work and work overload are, for some people some of the defining factors in their daily lives.

According to the American Stress Institute, researchers have estimated that 75 - 90 percent of all visits to primary care physicians are for problems related to stress.

Additionally, scientists have medically linked six leading causes of death to stress:

Cancer	Suicide
Heart Disease	Accidents
Lung Ailments	Cirrhosis of the Liver.

So what's the good news?

There are some simple techniques that you can start to use that can help you to manage and reduce the stress that you feel in the IB program and in life.

Understanding stress

Before I get into how to manage your stress, I want to talk a little bit about what stress is.

First, not all stress is bad for you. A certain degree of stress in your life will keep you driven and motivated to succeed. Live without stress and you might as well go meditate on a mountain top - life will be good, but very boring.

Too much stress will also kill you, so the secret lies in finding a good balance.

There are basically two types of stress that people feel: eustress and distress.

1. Eustress is what many call 'good stress'. This is stress that makes you work harder, the pressure that a big project or presentation brings on.

2. Distress is 'bad stress'. This is what kills you. Distress is the body reacting to a perceived threat. Too much eustress, like having too much of a good thing, eventually leads to distress.

    This is where the 'out of control' feeling comes from.

Life Management

There are several techniques that you can use to manage stress.

For the past 150 years or so, people have been using what is commonly known as 'time management'. This is a system where you manage everything that you have to do with a planner, to-do list, filling each one in by asking yourself "What do I need to do today?"

Over the years, hundreds of systems for time management have been developed, ranging from the simple to the extraordinarily complex and expensive.

While nothing is wrong with a good time management system, it's only the second half of the solution to getting rid of stress, anxiety, and problems like procrastination and caffeine overdosing that accompany them.

To really kick the habit, there is a more comprehensive system to managing your time and stress levels. I like to think of it as life-management.

Making Goals

The first part of life-management is not crazy or complex. It doesn't involve a complex system for organizing your locker, Tai Chi, or a digital planner that will text you homework assignments.

Instead, it starts with a simple question:

What do you really want?

What do you really want? Why are you here? Why do you want to receive an IB diploma?

It is a lot easier to get to where you want to go if you start off knowing where you want to end up. Many students who burn out of the diploma program do not fail for lack of smarts or ability. The quitters end up quitting because when the going gets tough, they have to make some tough decisions about what they're doing and how they are spending their time.

A little soul-searching often leads them to a place of "I'm just not good enough to do this" or "I'm not right for this" or "This is not who I want to be".

When you do not have a reason that drives you to persevere, it is hard to succeed, and all too easy to quit.

The IB Diploma program is tough; it has been designed to be a world-class education of the highest caliber. You are going to need some good reasons to get through it. You need to have goals.

Your goals don't have to be super elaborate or life changing. Making them simple will make it more likely that you will ultimately be able to achieve them.

What if you have no idea what you want or what your goals are?

First off, you would not be here, reading this if you did not have a reason to. Getting your goals down on paper is not that difficult; all you need to do is ask the right questions.

Lets break this down into a few simple steps. I recommend busting out some paper and a pen and answering a few questions to help define what you want and why you want it.

Right now.

Get some paper out right now. Your answers do not have to be perfect, just get something written down

Questions:

1. Why do you want to do the IB program?

   Are you in IB because you want to be or because your parents want you to be?

2. How committed are you to completing the IB?

3. Do you want to get a full diploma or just certificates?

4. What do you want to get out of the diploma program? What are your goals in IB?

   Do you want to be your school's valedictorian? A 4.0 GPA? Acceptance to an ivy-league school? A full ride scholarship? Just to get the diploma? Prove to yourself that you can do it?

For this last question, write out as many things as you can think of, numbering each item.

A goal without a reason is just a dream, so in the space below your list write down at least one reason why you absolutely must achieve that outcome.

Any reason will do, but the best reasons will be ones that get you excited, and motivated to do what you want to do.

If it's three in the morning and you have to finish a 10-page paper by first period, something like "I want to go to a good school" might not be enough to keep you going.

Personally, I need a reward, something like "To set myself up for incredible success while making my family proud of my accomplishments". That is something that resonates with me and something that I will work hard for.

Spend a few minutes thinking up some reasons that motivate you.

Seriously

Do not turn the page until you have answered every question and written down at least three outcomes you want to accomplish in the IB diploma program and reasons why you want to accomplish them.

Did you get at least two goals written down? If not, go back and do it right now. There is no time like the present.

Great.

That was the hardest part. Keep these goals & reasons handy; put them in the front of your binder, in your locker, or on the wall by your desk at home.

The next step is putting together a plan to make sure you achieve that success.

A good plan for success in the IB is defined by several elements. These include:

Classes and subject areas that you study, how many exams you sit for, what is offered at your school, and what level of the program you want to achieve.

As well, you may want to plan out things like your daily study times and a schedule for getting papers and projects completed.

Your game plan is simply an extension of your goals. It is the action plan that lets you achieve them, do not over think when you are making it. A game plan should be flexible and open to change whenever you or your goals change.

In general, however, the best way to get what you want in the IB diploma program is to be organized.

Organization

Planning

The first step to being organized is to implement a system to keep track of all of your due dates, assignments, notes, papers, and research. Start with getting a good planner.

I prefer to use one where there is space to write down your full assignments every day. Personally, I like the tangibility of a physical planner, but you may find that an online planner such as Google Calendar is much more flexible (especially if your school issues laptops). Either way, choose a planner that you like and find comfortable using on a daily basis.

In your planner, write down homework assignments and their due dates as well as any important dates for papers, projects, and exams. You may also want to write in holidays, dates with family and friends, and any extracurricular activities.

A planner is good for writing down daily assignments, but is especially useful in tracking long-term assignments. When you receive a large assignment, break it up into sections and plan when you are going to complete them. This goes a long way towards eliminating stress in IB.

Having a project planned and on track to being done ahead of time is much easier than trying to do everything in the few days, or pre-dawn hours before it is due.

> "If you fail to plan,

Scheduling

> ...you plan to fail"

After you know what things you need to do and when to do them, it is imperative to set aside enough time to get everything done. A consistent study/homework schedule will help you do better in classes along with saving a lot of time and stress.

There are two extremely important rules to remember when scheduling your time.

The first is the 80/20 rule, also known as Pareto's law. This is the idea that for many events, approximately 80% of the effects come from 20% of the causes.

The 80/20 rule means that you will do 80% of your work in 20% of the time that you have allotted to complete it.

The second rule to keep in mind when scheduling your time is that work expands to fill the time allotted. Essentially this means that if you have a 1500 word paper to write, and give yourself two weeks to write it, the paper will take you two weeks to write.

However, if you give yourself just three days to finish the paper, you will complete it in that time as well.

Of course, this example does have its extremes. Taking the necessary two days to thoroughly complete an essay will result in a higher grade than if you tried to complete that same assignment in less than an hour. Realize, however that a lot of work takes less time to complete than you may think it does.

Giving yourself only the absolute necessary time to complete it will make you more focused and efficient while reducing stress when you get your homework done earlier. I always try to challenge myself to get homework and projects done early and in less time. Use a countdown timer or a stopwatch and see how fast you can get it done!

The most important thing to do when you schedule your time for studying and homework is to develop a consistent daily schedule. Realize that you may not always be able to stick exactly by your schedule, I rarely do, but it will ultimately help you get more done by keeping what you have to do and when you need to do it on your mind.

Many students start making their schedule by first taking into account how much time it takes them to complete all of their daily assigned work, then adding time to work on big projects, study for tests, and adding in time for extracurricular activities and anything else that they have going on.

To Do Lists

Along with having a clear idea of when assignments are due, I find to-do lists essential. There are all sorts of ways to keep a to-do list. Some prefer small notebooks or binders, you may also want to consider an online to-do list tracker like **rememberthemilk. com** or **todoist.com**. Google's Gmail and Calendar also have a nice task list feature.

My personal standbys are sticky notes. Get the big wide ones so you can put them inside of your notebooks or planner.

Every day, use a sticky note to build a critical six. Write down the six most important tasks or assignments that you must complete that day. This will help you to remain focused on completing *the most essential tasks for right now* and not be distracted by the frightening list of five hundred things you have to finish in the next two weeks.

Taking Notes

Keeping your notes organized will go a long way in helping your sanity.

To start, find a notebook style that suits you. Personally I prefer multi-colored, single class, spiral bound notebooks. However many people also prefer lab notebooks or multi-class spiral-bound notebooks.

Either way, assign one notebook to each class that you take and label them clearly. Putting the class name and semester date on the cover will help you remember which notebook is which and using different colors for each class makes finding the right notebook super easy.

Organize your notes well. At the start of each class, session put down the date and use headings to mark topic changes. In class, copy down everything that the instructor writes down, and any important things that are spoken. It is also a good idea to write down any details on homework or projects in your notebook when you get them in class, as well as in your planner. This will ensure you never lose any important details or deadlines.

For homework that you write out, like math, get an extra notebook that you can tear pages out of or just a stack of ruled paper that is kept handy.

During class, you will tend to acquire a lot of loose papers. Keep track of them by getting a small (about 1") 3-ring binder. Get a set of dividers and file your papers as you receive them.

Study Areas

To make your studying effective, it is essential to have a good place to study. Ideally, you should set up a space that is free from regular distraction and will give you room to work. If you do not have a comfortable place to work and concentrate, you should do your best to find one.

A dedicated study space gives room to store all of your work, organize your assignments, and provides a refuge so that you can concentrate on what is important.

A computer is invaluable, you will need to write a LOT and often times submit assignments online. As well, computers are great for research. Desktop computers are great, but I prefer a laptop because they are super portable. You can take it to school, to friends' houses, the library, or wherever else you are going to study. If you do not have access to a computer, try to complete your typing and internet assignments at school or a public library.

Keep your desk relatively clean and organized. To help with all of the papers that you get set up a filing drawer where you can file things based on which class they are from and by categories such as tests, resources, homework, papers, etc.

Go through your locker and study areas at least once every term. Keeping old work out the way and filed will keep what you need at hand and make it easy to find something for reference when you need it.

I never throw anything out and I still have nearly every paper and homework assignment from IB sitting on my bookshelf in huge white three-ring binders. You never know when that stuff can come in handy, like when writing a book on the IB program!

Putting it all together

It is easy to blur the line between being efficient (doing a lot) and being effective (getting a lot done). A lot of students will spend hours smashing their head into a textbook or staring at a computer screen, and not have much to show for their time.

Eliminate wasted time by keeping yourself focused on what needs to be done. If you finish early, that is more time to do whatever you want to do. Ask yourself "Is what I am doing moving me closer to where I want to be?" If the answer is "No", you may want to re-evaluate what you are doing.

Beyond having goals, a schedule, and a clean work area, your survival in IB is dependent of developing good study habits and organization.

Re-evaluate your schedule from time to time; you will need to make changes in all of this until you find a system that works for you. Day to day however, follow the schedule that you set up and remember that you designed it. You are in IB because you want to be. Your success starts with doing what you set out to do when you need to do it and getting them done.

Procrastination

For some, the struggle against procrastination might be a daily battle. For others, procrastination may only rear its ugly head at the worst possible times. The danger of procrastination lies in the reality that it is so easy to slip into a habit of putting things off. However, once the ball is rolling, its effects can be irreversible.

In fact, procrastination is not only one of the biggest reasons candidates do not receive full IB diplomas, it can also be directly linked to much of the stress and any failure you will experience in the IB diploma program.

Kicking the habits of procrastination will help you reduce stress, get better grades, and have a lot more success.

Also, do not kid yourself. Everyone procrastinates on *something*. Putting something off until tomorrow is the easiest way to reduce stress and workload in the moment, especially if you have a tight schedule.

The problem arrives when putting things off becomes a habit, and nothing gets done on a daily basis. The end game comes when assignments are due; you are up all night furiously writing and studying. This is not a good plan if you want to create anything decent or retain knowledge.

Therefore, you must retrain yourself to not put anything off, to get things done as soon as possible, and on a consistent basis.

The reality is that building good habits takes time and practice, do not expect everything to work the first time. Like organization and study skills, getting rid of procrastination is something you will need to work on every day.

Kicking the Habit

There are only a couple of steps to elimination and the good news is that these steps are not all too radical or different from what you are doing right now. In fact, you may already know how to do most of them.

Step 1 is to start implementing the organization and management techniques that we talked earlier in the chapter. These techniques are the basis for success with your time and tasks in and out of the IB program.

They are the fundamentals that are critical to your success.

Step 2 is to follow the rules for setting and having goals. Most procrastination is caused by a lack of motivation.

By keeping good goals and reminding yourself of WHY you are doing something, WHY you want to do it (and not why you NEED to do it); the urge to procrastinate will begin to evaporate.

Step 3 is to get back to the organizational basics. Really. If you have properly planned your time, have goals, and are motivated to follow through, procrastination should never really appear on your radar.

If you find yourself stuck in the rut of procrastination and feel the walls starting to fold in, now is the perfect time to kick out of it.

Go and re-read the previous chapter on organization and goal setting. Build a massive action plan that directly addresses the situation you are in right now. Then start working.

After all, this is step four: **taking action**.

If you struggle with what you want to do, take action. It can be as simple as reading a chapter in your chemistry book or looking up resources to cite in your next paper. Even the smallest first step is still a step in the right direction.

8 ***Academic Survival***

Having goals, paying attention in class, and understanding how the IB program works will only get you so far. The diploma program runs off of studying, writing, and research.

So that's what this chapter is about. Use these next few sections to become an academic rock star and take school to the next level.

Research like a Pro

The ability to research topics in depth effectively is an essential skill in the IB diploma program. While every IB course involves some aspect of independent research, courses from group 3 and the extended essay are the most research-intensive sections of the diploma program.

There are two major types of research, primary and secondary investigations.

Primary research focuses on collecting new data or information that does not yet exist. This type of research is conducted through experiments by scientists or interviews by historians.

Secondary research focuses on the collection, summary, and synthesis of already existing information.

This section will focus on how to conduct secondary qualitative research with greater speed and accuracy.

Research is a time intensive process. Often, most of the time that is spent working on a paper or project is not spent actually producing the assignment, but in finding and organizing the information that is required to complete it.

Thus, good research skills cannot only make your assignments easier and quicker to complete; but better information and organization will ultimately lead you to better grades in your assignments and assessments.

Most likely you have already had some experience in research before entering the IB program. So instead of covering the basics in depth; we are going to dive right in, get our hands dirty, and talk about how to get good information *quickly and effectively*.

Have a purpose

One of the most important aspects of research in the IB is that it is purpose driven. You will always have something to find and a reason to find it. Knowing what your purpose is before you begin your research is essential if you want to find good information quickly.

> A purpose often will take the form of a topic or research question.

For most assignments, you may be given a general topic and then expected to create a thesis and subsequent paper or project. This can be extremely frustrating and many students spend HOURS just figuring out what to write about.

Things do not have to be so complicated. Instead of bashing your head into a computer screen; make life easier by focusing your ideas and what you look up.

Start by doing some quick Google searches on your assigned subject or topic. Find something in the field that interests you.

Next, narrow down the focus of your assignment until you have something manageable and interesting.

> For example, instead of writing about how the civil rights movement impacted American culture, focus your topic and write about the historical significance of Martin Luther King's "I Have a Dream" speech and its impact on Dr. King's movement.

The purpose for your research does not have to be complicated or original; it only needs to be descriptive and specific. This ensures that you will only be collecting information that is relevant to your investigation.

Additionally, it is important to be sure that the subject you choose to research is in line with your assignment. Researching a paper that you cannot turn in is probably not a good use of your time and energy.

Finding Sources

There are a lot of different techniques for gathering information. I have a personal favorite few however that I always use and that tend to work very well.

Online

Google is your best friend. As of 2008, Google engineers reported that they had indexed approximately 1 trillion web pages. Along with a remarkable search engine, Google also has engines for searching through books and scholarly journals.

I always start my research with a Google search to get relevant information and find a good list of sources to look into later.

Another great way to start is Wikipedia. Wikipedia articles sometimes get a bad rap for being inaccurate and unprofessional. While you should definitely never cite a Wikipedia article in your final report or rely on it as a primary source, Wikipedia is a fantastic way to get a good overview of a subject quickly.

Additionally, Wikipedia articles tend to be specific, give links to other relevant articles, and often contain a list of both online and offline resources that were used in writing the article.

These resources you can use and they are an excellent place to start finding great information. I have completed several projects using only the primary sources I found through Wikipedia articles.

In addition to Wikipedia and Google, many schools have subscriptions to scholarly journal sites such as JSTOR. Especially for scientific or very technical topics, these directories can be fantastic resources that allow access to information that would be otherwise impossible to find.

Offline

Away from the internet, there are several ways to find good information. Unless you have an amazing and extensive school library, I would not recommend using it. For the most part, high school libraries will only offer a cursory overview of what is available.

Depending on where you live, city or county libraries can be great places to do research. Get a library card if you do not have one already (they are free by the way), and use a computer terminal to find relevant books or articles on your topic. Again, it can be helpful to do a Google search to get an idea of what type of materials you are looking for.

If your local library system has more than one branch, your best bet in most cases will be to go to the main or largest branch. In Seattle, the central library is enormous and provides an excellent research location not only for finding information, but also for reading and writing.

As good as a local library may be they often cannot hold a candle to the resources that are available at a university library. If you live close to a large university, the library is undoubtedly worth a visit.

When you go, make sure to bring cash and coin for photocopies as most universities do not allow anyone but their students to check out library materials. Once you are there, use a public access computer to find what you need.

At larger universities, there usually exist specialized libraries for certain departments and often, these yield the best resources. No matter how obscure your subject, chances are high that someone has written a thesis paper on it (I have found thesis papers on the finer details of alpine ski construction). If you can find a good thesis paper, use it and its sources for high quality, original information.

Organization

As you begin to gather information, it can be easy to get overwhelmed with what you find. Information overload is easy to create and hard to escape from when you actually sit down to write.

In order to keep track of what you need to find and what you have already, use a four-step system:
1. Define
2. Locate
3. Notate
4. Organize

Do not worry, it is not as complicated as it may initially seem.

The first step is to define what you are looking for. This should not be too hard; you have already done it when you created a topic. However, it is important to be more specific. Break up your topic into sub-categories you want to talk about. In essence, start to create a rough outline of what you want your report to look like.

The outline does not have to be anywhere close to perfect, start with a list of what things you want to cover in your report and go from there.

Next, you need to locate the information. Use Google, Wikipedia, or the library.

To save time, gather every resource that you think will be relevant. Then skim through, taking note of what pages you think you will need. Finally, photocopy everything you find relevant at one time (including the copyright page for citations) and review the material in depth later.

As you come across information, take care to keep everything organized. Keep a note pad and your outline in front of you and write down ideas and where you found them as you do your research.

In the same way, you may find it helpful to keep a document open on your computer into which you past whole parts of websites while you browse the internet for information.

Alternatively, there is a great website to make this easier called **evernote.com**, which will 'clip' all or part of a website for you and organize it for viewing later in online notebooks. The site is free and even offers a Firefox browser plug-in that makes recording relevant information when you browse the web easy and efficient.

Organize your photocopies and web articles into folders both on and off line. I like to use stickies, colored tabs, and a highlighter to keep track of what is important.

You may also want to consider getting a three ring binder that is devoted to your project in order to store all of the documents you gather. Put everything together in the order of your project outline so that it will be easy to find what you need when you start to write

Ultimately, research is always sort of a messy process. It is fumbling through a dark room looking for the light switch. You may blunder along for a while, and as you go, you will become more and more refined in your search until finally, you flip the switch and everything comes clear.

So do not despair if a project looks overwhelming, if you break it down and have a goal, you will be ready to tackle the meanest of research projects.

Writing Outstanding Papers & Essays

Writing is something that you will do a lot of in the IB. Almost every IB course expects students to express their research and ideas concisely, accurately, and clearly in writing.

Your writing assignments will take the form of either a paper or an essay.

Essays are shorter pieces of work, usually a page or two in length and incorporate the author's opinions and thoughts.

Papers are usually longer than essays and present analytical and critical analysis of a particular topic.

Both formats must be clearly organized, well thought out, and strategically composed.

Beyond this basic distinction, there are four basic types of writing in IB:

1. Research papers
2. Literary and expository essays
3. Persuasive, argumentative essays
4. Narrative, descriptive or response essays and papers

So, what is the difference between all of these?

The biggest difference between them lies in their content. The actual process of writing a paper or an essay is essentially the same, regardless of its content or format.

Every piece of writing you create will have a topic, main argument, supporting statements, and a conclusion.

Of course, not every paper can fit into a cookie cutter mold; a research paper will require time to research and cite facts, while a persuasive essay may be based solely off personal opinion.

The research paper uses facts to support a conclusion, while a persuasive essay convinces the reader to adopt a particular viewpoint with the help of supporting examples.

Steps

When you come down to it, each writing assignment is relatively the same. There are eight essential steps which go into writing a solid paper or essay:

1. Define a topic & focus
2. Brainstorm and organize your ideas
3. Create a concise thesis statement
4. Outline what you want to talk about
5. Write the main body, one section at a time
6. Solidify the introduction and conclusion
7. Proof read and correct

8. Reorganize and rewrite and proof again as necessary

First, get some definition to your writing.

In order to write, you must have a topic. For most writing assignments, you will be given a general subject or a specific topic to write about. In the case of the extended essay, you will not be given a topic at all and must first figure out what exactly you want to write about.

Whether you have a topic or not, it is important to make the paper interesting and relevant to you. Never write a paper just because you have to.

If you are interested and invested in what you are writing about, your paper will be easier to write and definitely score a higher grade.

After you have a topic figured out, you need to make sure that it is refined and specific enough to fit your assignment. It is easy to start a paper or an essay with a broad topic and become quickly overwhelmed figuring out what to include in your writing.

Make things easier from the start by choosing a specific focus for your writing.

While the focus of a large research paper will definitely be more broad than that of a one page response essay; your focus, regardless of the format, should address only one or two specific ideas or questions within a topic.

Second, brainstorm for a bit when figuring out exactly what you want to talk about.

This is one of the most important parts of your writing. If you have an interesting, specific, and relevant focus to your writing, what you need to say should come to you easily and quickly.

Third, just start writing. I know it sounds dumb, but just getting something down is a tested and proven way to work out your paper.

Begin with a note pad and jot anything and everything that comes to mind when you think about your topic. Write down what things you want to focus on, what ideas seem most interesting.

Once you have a good idea of what exactly you want to write about, synthesise this into a thesis statement so a reader can easily understand what you are talking about.

You should have some sort of thesis statement for every paper that you write. The thesis does not have to be long or complicated, just enough to concisely sum up what you intend to say or prove in your writing.

Writing It

With your thesis statement in hand, it is time to write. If you have a super short essay and a good idea of what you are going to cover, there is no problem with just starting.

Personally however, I like to put together an outline for everything that I write.

An outline keeps all of your ideas organized and makes your paper relevant and readable. It also makes it easier to write. Depending on the complexity and length of your paper or essay, your outline may vary in length, and be more or less detailed.

At the very least, an outline should be a list of the major sections of your paper including the introduction and conclusion. To make the outline more complete, include a list of each specific thing you are going to talk about in each section of your paper.

A complete outline will include not only the topics covered in each section, but it will be broken down so that the subject of each sentence or paragraph is listed.

This makes writing a snap, because you already know what you are going to say for each sentence or paragraph that you write.

If your goal is to get a good grade, it is important to keep your writing clearly structured. So every paper or essay you write should include:

- An introduction with a clear statement on what the paper is about.
- A body with sections that define, argue, and support the main point.
- A conclusion that concisely restates the main points and supporting arguments or discovery that was made.

You may choose to write the introduction and conclusion after you have written the main body of the paper.

Once you have your paper written, it is much easier to summarize the main points in the beginning and end. Additionally, this can cut down on your final editing because you will not have to constantly revise these sections.

Banishing writer's block

Your papers and essays are not being graded on the time that you spend writing them. Without a doubt, writing a good essay takes some time. However, this process can be accomplished much quicker and easier than you may think.

When you sit down to write, make sure to find a place that is comfortable and easy to work in. Put on some nice music and focus on writing, even if you are just staring at a blank screen.

Writers block comes to everyone, the trick to beating it is to let go of your inhibitions and write whatever comes to mind. Even if you think what you are writing is garbage; it can always be edited later.

If you are still having trouble getting something down, try some B.S. to get your mind started. Check out chapter six for guidance on exactly how to do it.

Remember: whatever you write, you can always change it. Many people take a long time to write even a sentence because they try to make it perfect the first time.

Get over yourself and just put down whatever comes into your head. Believe me; editing is a lot easier once you have words on the page.

Devil in the Details

So you sat down, wrote for hours, and you are ready to hit print and turn everything.

Sure many IB students, myself included have turned in papers without ever reading them, sometimes just minutes after they finish writing them. In IB, these were the papers I always did the worst on.

So wait just a second before you hit print, you are not ready quite yet. Even the best first draft needs a little bit of TLC before its ready to become an A paper.

Remember how the topic and organization was a big part of writing a great paper? Well, the other important part of writing a great paper is the writing itself.

The first time you write your ideas down, there are bound to be mistakes in both what you say and how you say it.

It is important to set aside time to edit your paper thoroughly. Getting the words out is only the beginning and you can make or break a grade with editing.

There are six things to check for when you read over your first draft.

1. Spelling
2. Grammar
3. Relevance
4. Continuity and flow
5. Clarity
6. Citations and quotations

First, look for spelling and grammar.

If you are using a modern word processor like Microsoft Word, this is already done for you. While word is a powerful tool, you should adjust the settings for its grammar check to properly edit your paper.

Go into the preferences for spelling and grammar, and then change the grammar settings to check for both grammar & style. This lets word correct not just basic grammar and spelling, but also all the little things that pull down your grade like passive sentences and split infinitives.

As an added measure, read over your paper manually for grammar and spelling mistakes. Do not base your hard-earned grade on technology alone.

Next, read your thesis statement. Then, one by one, read each paragraph in your paper. Does each paragraph relate and/or support your main argument?

If a paragraph does not contribute to your paper, consider removing it. If you have several paragraphs that do not relate, consider modifying your thesis statement so that your paper is congruent.

As you read over each section, imagine that you are reading your work for the first time. Imagine you are your instructor and grade yourself.

How well does your paper read? Is it easy to follow the main ideas from one section to the next? How well do the sections and paragraphs flow together? Is it easy to understand and follow? Does everything make sense?

At this point, you may find yourself thinking that the paper would work better if it were put in a different order. This is totally OK and you should feel free reorganizing as much as you need to.

When your paper is clear and easy to read, read it again. Look at it quickly. Is it easy to ascertain the main ideas from the first few lines? Is it easy to read? If you were looking at it for the first time, would you want to read it?

If you can answer yes to these questions, than you are in good shape.

Finally, you want to thoroughly check your paper for citations and quotations. Make sure to put anything which you quoted in quotes and cite all of your sources. Include a bibliography for every piece of writing you do, no matter how small.

If you only have a small essay, include your bibliography in the footnotes. Make sure to cite all of your sources in a standardized format such as MLA or APA.

A neat trick to get your sources organized quickly is to use an online citation program such as easybib.com or bibme.org, both of which automatically format and organize your bibliography.

Remember that writing papers and essays is not hard, but it is a skill. The more times that you have to sit down and put your thoughts and ideas onto paper, the better at it you will get.

Eventually, writing may come naturally, maybe you are lucky and it already does. Either way, the secret to writing great papers and essays is to organize, get started, and proof thoroughly.

Hitting the Books

One of the biggest differences between the IB diploma program and any other advanced high school curriculum is its focus. Rather than focusing solely on learning information, IB courses are designed to teach **understanding** of concepts and principles and to know **how** to think and learn.

The diploma program wants to see it's students actively thinking and solving problems, not just remembering information.

Some people see this as making the IB diploma easier than traditional programs such as AP, and they argue that it means students do not have to actually study as much.

This could not be farther from the truth. As an IB student, you may not always need to know a plethora of memorized fact, however in order to achieve passing marks, it is imperative that you completely understand concepts beyond simply knowing information.

Studying in the IB is not something to take lightly. Many diploma candidates get caught up in the day-to-day work, and never take the time to **truly study**. Instead, they only hit the books in a few hectic weeks before exams in May.

This is cramming and rote memorization, not learning. Cramming is not the ideal way to learn the complex and varied concepts in IB. If you want to achieve high scores in your exams and get a diploma, you must study consistently and thoroughly.

Additionally, developing solid study skills early on will make a huge difference as to your success in university and beyond the IB program.

Habits and Space

The first key to effective studying is to make it a habit. Studying should be something that you do on a regular basis without fail.

For SL courses, try to study at least 3 hours per week for each course.

For HL courses, aim to study 5-6 hours per week for each course.

Note that this is independent study and exam prep outside of the normal coursework.

All this studying may sound like a lot to do, but if you are taking 5 IB courses at one time, 3 HL and 2 SL, you will only be studying about 3 hours per day on top of your regular course work.

Set up a study schedule so that you can block your study time and study only one or two classes per day. This means that for HL classes, you may study 2 hours three times per week for each class, and for SL courses you would study 1 hour, three times per week for each class.

Regardless of how you choose to set up your schedule, regular study habits will ensure that you really know the material and concepts. Consistency is essential; many of the ideas and concepts in IB courses take time to learn. Even if you cannot devote a lot of hours to studying outside of class, taking baby steps every day will ultimately net you much higher scores than trying to learn everything in the sparse weeks before the exams.

Find a study space where you can be without distraction. Organize your space, including with a reading light, room to read and an easy way to take notes. When you study, it may be best not to use a computer unless you find it necessary.

In most cases, a computer will be more prove to be distracting than helpful. The Internet offers a plethora of distractions and time wasters. It is ridiculously easy to waste 3 or 5 hours on Facebook, but if all you have is your books and a note pad, you will learn a lot more and get things done faster.

Reading

In 2003, an investigation into adult literacy in the United States by the National Center for Educational Statistics reported that at least 40% of the American population could only read at a 'basic' or 'below basic' literacy level.

To clarify, basic literacy means that at most a person is able to use a television guide to find out when programs are on, read and understand basic informational pamphlets, and compare ticket prices to two events. Most of the group actually reads below this level.

The same study found that only 13% of Americans read at a 'proficient' level.

The disparity in education and income between these two groups is massive.

Is being able to read important? Absolutely. Your ability to read and comprehend complex information quickly and accurately is essential to not only surviving, but also getting high marks in IB.

If you do not consider yourself a proficient reader, do not worry. Like most things, reading improves with practice.

In IB, there are two main types of materials to read:

1. Prose.
   This includes novels, short stories, articles and poems.

2. Technical Material.
   This includes textbooks, scholarly journal articles, and scientific data.

You will have a lot of reading to do in IB. Therefore, it is important to develop the reading skills necessary to be able to understand quickly what the material is saying.

Reading faster will not only make it easier to study, but also will help cut down on the time it takes to research and write papers and essays.

There are several things that you can do immediately to increase your reading speed and comprehension:

1. Expand your vocabulary. The more exposure you have to new words and difficult reading material the better.

   Instead of watching the news on TV, buy a copy of The Wall Street Journal or The New York Times and read with a notepad and a dictionary; whenever you find a word that you do not understand, write it down and look up the meaning.

2. Have a reason to read. If you know WHY you are reading something, it is easier to find the information that you are looking for.

   Before you start reading, have a clear idea of what exactly you want to learn from the text. If you have a list of questions that you must answer from the text, read the list over before you read, then keep it in front of you to remind yourself what you are looking for.

3. Skim before you read. Scanning the paragraph or section you are about to read is a great way to give your brain a snapshot of what you are about to read. This will help you move through sections faster and remember more.

4. Take notes. When you are reading anything that you will have to answer questions on, or write about later, keep a notepad with you and write down any important information.

   This will not only make writing easier later on, but writing things down has been proven to help learning and memory.

5. Organize and Prioritize. You cannot read everything all at once. The pressure to finish several chapters and novels for class can be just as overwhelming as research and writing.

   Set aside time for your reading and prioritize what you need to read and when you need to read it.

6. Focus. Once you start reading, do not stop. Set a reading goal and keep reading until you achieve it. For novels, set a bookmark 10-30 pages ahead and do not stop until you reach it.

   If you lose interest or keep losing your place, take a break and read something else.

7. Have a good place to read. Reading is an important part of studying. Make sure you have a quiet place without distractions so you can learn.

8. Read before bed. Before you go to sleep, read over your notes, read a chapter from a novel or textbook, read something.

Reading school material before going to sleep not only will make you tired and give you better sleep, your mind will also process the material while you sleep, helping you to learn more.

Do all the Problems in the Book

It takes time and practice to learn material. One of the biggest reason students do not score higher on their IB exams is that they do not take the steps necessary to actually learn the material for the exam.

There is a difference between learning and memorization. Learning means that you understand the core concepts and principles of the subject while memorization is just the ability to regurgitate facts.

IB exams test for learning, comprehension, and creative thinking; not how well you know dates and figures. The exams require that students show true understanding of a subject.

When studying for your exams, prepare by doing as many practice exams as you can find. Complete more problems in the book than you are assigned. Instead of only doing odd or even problems for a math chapter, do every problem in the chapter.

Working through every possible scenario in a subject is without a doubt the absolute best way to prepare for the IB exams. This over-preparation is the key to scoring high marks.

Studying for the test

Since your scores in IB are 70% - 80% dependent on how well you do on your exams; it only makes sense to structure your studying and review towards the exams.

Probably the nicest thing about the IB exams is that they are very structured.

While it is impossible to know exactly what each question will be, you can get a pretty good idea what topics are covered by each part of an IB exam.

Begin your exam preparation by taking a few practice tests and seeing how well you do on them. This will give you an idea of what areas of each subject you are strong at and on what things you need to improve. The content and structure of exams may change from year to year so it is important to also talk to your teachers or IB coordinator and get the mark schemes for the exams that you will be taking.

Next, structure your studying to incorporate all of the topics covered in the mark scheme for each exam.

You can get sample tests and examples of past exams from your teacher or IB coordinator. When you practice taking them, try to simulate the test-taking environment as accurately as possible.

In a real IB exam, you will only have a limited amount of time to finish and no access to any textbooks or the internet.

Practice your exams the way you will take them and you will have an easy time finding areas for improvement and score higher when you actually take the test.

Additionally, simulating the stress, pressure, and time constraints of taking an exam will help you learn to handle the pressure that the IB exams can create. This will help you to be prepared and calm when have to perform.

Getting down to brass tacks

The pressure is on; its mid-April and your first exams are looming on the horizon. May is a time that fills most IB students with an overwhelming sense of stress and dread. Over a short few weeks, months of work will all cumulate in a few hours of performance.

What do you need to know and how do you make sure that you are prepared?

The first step is to relax. Ultimately, you will do as well in your IB examinations as you deserve to do. If you have spent the months and years prior to your exams preparing and studying, you will do well. If your preparation might have left something to be desired, this is no time to throw in the towel; there are several ways to improve your memory and cram your way to a higher grade.

Without a doubt, waiting until the last possible moment to learn and prepare for an IB examination is not the best way to high scores. However, working hard at the last moment, regardless of your preparation before, can give you enough to pass.

Get the mark schemes for the tests you are going to be taking. Look over what you have to do.

What main concepts and ideas does the exam focus on? What sections of the test are worth the most points?

These are the sections that you want to focus on studying.

Make a check list of the concepts and topics that you need to know, then, one by one go through your list making note cards (you can also use a notebook) of the basic ideas and what you need to know for each topic.

Do this at least once, twice if you can. Try to memorize the core ideas and facts behind each subject and topic. Remember that the IB exams are not so much about fact, but rather about how well you understand concepts and principles.

If you can remember how something works, the small details are not so important.

When you sit down to the examination, relax. You have done a lot of work to get there. Enjoy your exams; they are an opportunity to show just how much you know.

Staying Motivated and Energized

Studying and preparing for you IB classes and exams is mentally and physically exhausting. Use organization and routine to keep your fire burning throughout the year and only cram when it is absolutely necessary. It is also important to set aside time to do something besides IB.

Keep yourself active by playing a sport or participating in other extracurricular activities. Studying 24/7 is not healthy and if you don't take time out for yourself, you will not only feel horrible and go crazy, you will not do as well in classes and in exams.

Eating and sleeping right are essential. Make your sleeping schedule a regiment and try to wake up at the same time every day. You do not need a full 9 hours of sleep every night, but try to get at least 7 hours. Anything below five or six hours will start to lead to fatigue and memory loss.

Stay motivated by focusing on your goals. Give yourself a reason to fight. If you know why you are waking up every morning, going to class, then studying for five hours every night, you will be invested and interested in what you are doing.

If the idea of getting an IB diploma does not excite you, find something that does or forget about doing the IB altogether.

Do not slack through the diploma program. This is for those who want a challenge and who want to win. If you are motivated and energized, stay focused on the goal and your success in IB will come.

9 ***Academic Honesty***

Academic honesty is a serious matter for both you and the IB.

You may be wondering;

> "Why do I need to know about academic honesty? I am a decent and honest person. I would never steal or cheat."

While I know that you probably are a respectful, good human being, there are some rules and concepts of academic honesty that do not always follow common sense. Some of the concepts of academic honesty you may of never even considered before.

It important to know what constitutes academic honesty mainly for your own protection. The IB takes this issue very seriously.

Students who violate the IB's terms of academic honesty face harsh and swift penalties that range from have certain pieces of work invalidated to being dismissed from the IB program and possibly their school.

Additionally, the damage of being suspended from IB over academic honesty does not always stop in high school. Students dismissed or accused of cheating and plagiarism can lose scholarships and even be denied entrance to university.

While this is really a worst-case scenario and most students never have any run in with the harsh hand of IB, most problems relating to academic honesty are easily preventable with a little bit of knowledge and common sense.

What does academic honesty mean?

Essentially, academic honesty means that all of your academic work is produced with integrity, independently, and according to established guidelines of conduct.

Any type of academic dishonesty is referred to in the IB as malpractice.

There are two major and common types of malpractice: plagiarism and collusion.

Plagiarism

To give a complete definition of what plagiarism is and is not, I will let plagiarism.org explain:

"Many people think of plagiarism as copying another's work, or borrowing someone else's original ideas. However, terms like "copying" and "borrowing" can disguise the seriousness of the offense:

According to the Merriam-Webster Online Dictionary, to "plagiarize" means

- To steal and pass off (the ideas or words of another) as one's own
- To use (another's production) without crediting the source
- To commit literary theft
- To present as new and original an idea or product derived from an existing source.

In other words, plagiarism is an act of fraud. It involves both stealing someone else's work and lying about it afterward.

> But can words and ideas really be stolen?

According to U.S. law, the answer is yes. The expression of original ideas is considered intellectual property, and is protected by copyright laws, just like original inventions. Almost all forms of expression fall under copyright protection as long as they are recorded in some way (such as a book or a computer file).

All of the following are considered plagiarism:

- Turning in someone else's work as your own
- Copying words or ideas from someone else without giving credit
- Failing to put a quotation in quotation marks
- Giving incorrect information about the source of a quotation
- Changing words but copying the sentence structure of a source without giving credit
- Copying so many words or ideas from a source that it makes up the majority of your work, whether you give credit or not.

Most cases of plagiarism can be avoided, however, by citing sources. Simply acknowledging that certain material has been borrowed, and providing your audience with the information necessary to find that source, is usually enough to prevent plagiarism. See our section on citation for more information on how to cite sources properly."

FROM WWW·PLAGARISM·ORG

Additionally, the IB acknowledges that most cases of plagiarism which are prosecuted do not arise as result of deliberate malpractice, but rather stem from the student not properly acknowledging or citing sources.

It is essential that you acknowledge give every source and quote that you use in writing papers and essays for IB. For more information on citations, see chapter 8.

Collusion

Collusion is an easy trap to fall into for many students. Collusion is defined as helping another student in his or her malpractice. Allowing your work to be copied or another student to turn in your work as their own is considered collusion.

A common example of collusion often starts simply and friendly:

Let's say that Jimmy has spent the last two weeks writing

his final essay and it is due tomorrow. Sally has been procrastinating and has barely written anything. Not know what to do, she asks Jimmy if she can borrow a copy of his paper to inspire her writing.

Late into the night fueled by stress and caffeine, Sally decides that she cannot possibly finish everything on time and so she copies the outline and a large portion of Jimmy's paper.

When they are both caught, Sally gets in trouble for plagiarism and Jimmy is busted for collusion. What started out as a friendly gesture has now turned ugly.

Being a good friend and helping people is never a bad thing, however you must use caution when sharing what you have done with other Diploma candidates.

Duplication & Other Types of Malpractice

Beyond plagiarism or collusion, duplication is something that many IB candidates do not consider. It is malpractice to resubmit work for more than one assessment component or diploma requirement.

This means that the amazing essay you wrote for your philosophy internal assessment CANNOT be turned in as a TOK essay.

There are additional specific circumstances that the IB considers malpractice. I have listed them here for your benefit.

In addition to collusion and plagiarism, a student is in malpractice if they:

- Duplicate work to meet the requirements of more than one assessment component
- Fabricate data for an assignment
- Take unauthorized material into an examination room
- Disrupt an examination by an act of misconduct, such as distracting another candidate
- Exchange, support, or attempt to support, the passing on of information that is or could be related to the examination
- Fail to comply with the instructions of the invigilator or other member of the school's staff responsible for the conduct of the

examination
- Impersonate another candidate
- Steal examination papers
- Disclose or discuss the content of an examination paper with a person outside the immediate school community within 24 hours after the examination
- Use an unauthorized calculator during an examination.

FROM THE IB HANDBOOK OF PROCEDURES

Academic Infringement

There may be a circumstance where a candidate submits a work and makes a small mistake; not citing a source or forgetting to out a quote in quotation marks.

If the candidate has made it clear that they acknowledge the ideas and resources they used, but were negligent in citation, the final award committee may rule the case academic infringement.

Academic infringement is not considered malpractice and is only applicable in a case where a candidate made accidental mistake and did not attempt to gain an unfair advantage.

In this case, a candidate is still eligible for a grade in the subject as well as the IB diploma. It is likely however that the component or part of the component in question will be discarded and not graded.

What to do if you f*&! Up

OK, so things got messy and the hammer is starting to come down. What do you do now?

There are several actions that you can take to improve your current situation and your eventual outcome.

The first thing is that every case of academic dishonesty or malpractice is treated on a case-by-case basis by the IB and by the school.

There are rules and consequences for malpractice; however, there is no cookie cutter situation. The IB treats every situation of malpractice as unique.

Thus, approach an accusation of malpractice with honesty and an open mind. In general do not lie or attempt to deceive anyone in your school or associated with the IB in any way, what so ever.

Regardless of circumstances, you are already suspected of dishonesty, so further deception will not be beneficial to your situation.

How big is the problem?

You know that an accusation of malpractice is without a doubt your problem. The next step towards resolution is the determination if the issue is going to be handled by the IB or by your school.

To help guard against malpractice, the IB requires that a signed cover sheet accompany every material that is turned in with every assessment, whether internal or external. This cover sheet states that all of the work being submitted is the sole work of the candidate and has been created by them alone.

Standard procedure dictates that if an instance of malpractice is discovered BEFORE this cover sheet is signed; a resolution of the malpractice issue is up to the school. In this case you should consult with your school as every school's policy for dealing with malpractice will be different.

Mitigation

In the case that the malpractice is discovered after you have signed the cover sheet and submitted the work, the IB deals with the issue.

The IB has a set of rules and proceedings for how they handle malpractice.

In general, the process proceeds in three stages:

First, the IB coordinator at the school, as well as the IBCA (International Baccalaureate Curriculum and Assessment Centre), is notified of the issue. This includes written documentation from the school and coordinator.

Along with this statement, the candidate(s) in question may submit their own statement in response to the allegation to the IBCA in order to better document the incident.

It should be noted that, you as a student have a right to view all of the accusations and evidence against you, as well as to be informed if you are under investigation for malpractice.

Next, if there is basis for an investigation; the IBCA will instruct the coordinator to conduct an investigation, which consists of a statement from the teacher for the subject concerned, the coordinators own statement, a statement from the candidate, and a summary of an interview with the candidate about the allegation of malpractice.

Finally, upon completion of this report, the case is presented to the final award committee. This committee will review all of the presented evidence and has full discretion to decide whether to dismiss the accusation, uphold it and assign an appropriate penalty, or to request further investigation.

Reconsideration and Appeal

In the case that the committee does uphold an accusation, a candidate has the right to request a reconsideration of the committee's decision.

This is only possible if the candidate is able to produce and establish facts that were unknown when the original decision was made.

An additional appeal is possible as well, but only on the grounds that the procedures defined in the IB Regulations, which led to the final decision of the case in question, were not properly followed.

In general, both of these circumstances are difficult, though not impossible to achieve once a final decision has been reached.

Ultimately, the best solution for malpractice is prevention. This starts in vigilance and an awareness of the possibilities and existence of academic dishonesty.

Remember that academic dishonesty is real and present. It is not something to be taken lightly in the IB program.

If you do the right thing and are aware, you should have no problem.

Afterwards

To boldly go where no one has gone
before!

                    -James T. Kirk

10 ***Getting In: College & Beyond***

Perhaps one of the biggest reasons that students endure the challenges of the IB diploma program is university. The doors that the IB opens up in terms of higher education are numerous.

Admissions officers know about the IB program and its academic demands. Colleges admire the skills that IB develops in its students and many actively recruit IB students. If you don't have a duffel bag full of college mail yet, don't worry, you probably will soon.

With an IB diploma, candidates can competitively apply to top US schools as well as schools abroad. Depending on their scores, many diploma candidates are able to receive college credit based off the work they have done in the IB program.

Why Go

The benefits of higher education are clear. College graduates have exponentially more job opportunities than people who do not pursue any education beyond high school.

According to collegeboard.com, college graduates have higher quality jobs and make at least $20,000 a year more than those who stop their educations at high school.

Going to college is not only an opportunity to set yourself up for the future but also a time to grow personally and academically.

Even better, the IB program is considered to be one of the absolute best college prep programs in the world and an IB diploma will put you in the perfect place for the academic demands of college.

Admissions

The process of getting into college begins at least a year before you graduate high school.

Spend time researching where you want to go. Look at academic programs, locations, reputation, and price. Every school is different and offers something unique.

Consider which colleges you want to apply to carefully, however if you are not 100% set on a particular school, that is OK. It is better to have choice later on than to be without options. If you truly hate a particular university once you get there - it's always possible to transfer.

How many colleges should you apply to? It depends on your grades, where you want to go, and your SAT, ACT, and IB scores.

Even if you opt for early admission, its best to have applied to LEAST one back up school that you wouldn't mind going too if all else fails. On the other side of this coin, there are students that apply to 25, 30, or more colleges to increase their chances of being accepted. Honestly, this approach is a complete waste of money.

The best approach to college applications is to apply at 1-2 "dream" schools. These are universities where you would really like to go, but may be a little beyond your abilities or extremely difficult to get into. Also apply at 2-3 "hopeful" schools, universities where you are pretty confident you will be accepted. Finally, apply to 1-2 "backup" schools, universities or colleges where you are sure to be accepted, just in case.

Time and money

Remember that every college application takes time and money. Besides the fees for tests like the SAT and ACT, you also have to pay for each application.

More importantly, many top schools require a pretty stringent array of essays, questions, forms, and interviews. Expect to spend at the very least 3-5 hours on each application.

If you are applying to 10 colleges, this can mean several days of work. Coupled with the time needed to prepare and take the standard college admission tests, your time to complete what you need to in IB can be severely strained.

Additionally, many college applications are due in the fall, right as the extended essay, TOK paper, and other major IB assignments are due.

A lot of students look to early admission to help with this problem. Some universities allow applicants to submit an application and receive a response to their acceptance before the fall of their senior year in college.

This can be a great relief. You know if and where you are going to college and you can apply during the summer before school even begins.

The only drawback of this is that it severely limits your application options. Most early admission offers include a clause that if you are accepted, you MUST by law attend the university following high school. So you if you apply early, be sure you REALLY want to go to the school.

Another way to help ease the load is to use a standardized application such as the common application. This application can be used at over 391 colleges in 42 states. It is given fair consideration along with the universities' proprietary application and greatly simplifies the hassle of writing out a separate college application for every school you apply to.

The best asset to your university admission is time. Plan ahead so that you have time to complete all of the applications on time and still keep up your grades in the IB.

Starting early is the best solution to solving the mess of college admission. Having application essays written and forms filled out before school starts in the fall will ultimately increase your chances of getting in as well as keeping your stress level down and your grades in IB up.

College Credit

Beyond the preparation and competitive edge that the IB gives, doing well in IB exams can pay off huge in college. As the IB is more and more recognized in the US and abroad, many universities offer transfer equivalency credits to students based on their work and their exam scores in IB.

At some universities, students can receive the equivalent of a year in credits for their work in the IB program.

Additionally, IB courses may allow a student to be placed in more advanced courses when starting a university.

All of this means that completing IB with high scores can shorten the time it takes to receive certain degrees at a university.

While each university has its own policy on awarding credits for IB scores; the majority only will award credits for subjects that are taken at the higher level and many require scores of a 5 or above in order to receive any credit at all.

A few schools such as Harvard University give credit to students in the form of "advanced standing". Harvard requires a score of 7 in at least three IB subjects.

As the IB policy of each university varies, it is important to check with the institutions that you are applying to for an accurate report of what is offered.

Notifying your University

In order to receive credit for your work in IB, you must officially notify your university of what your IB scores are. The IB takes care of this internally for you with the Request for Results service.

After you have finished the IB program, you are allowed to send your results to only one school or application institution in the USA, two in Canada, and a maximum of six worldwide.

Requests for the service must be submitted by the 1st of July to the IB by your program coordinator.

11 ***Getting Out***

Getting into IB is not too difficult. If you can read and write and are ready to tackle high school at the knees, you are ready to get started in the diploma program.

By now, you have probably managed to muddle through the first year or so and things are going swell. However, it is getting down to senior year and as the pressure starts to mount, you start to question your sanity, and your exit plan.

So, how do you get out of IB? More importantly, how do you get out of IB with your sanity, a college acceptance letter, and a snazzy diploma in your hand?

Going into your senior year, the most important thing to have is a plan. You are going to have a lot to get done. If you have a real, workable plan it will be much easier. Look back at chapter 7 if you do not have one yet.

At the very least, your plan should incorporate:

- Major projects, their timelines, and due dates
- College application timelines and due dates
- A checklist of IB diploma requirements and high school graduation requirements (see the appendix)

Hopefully, the IB program at your school is well managed, so what you need to do and when you need to do it is pretty well laid out.

Keep in mind that as you move towards graduation, you need to complete both the requirements for high school graduation as well as those for you IB diploma. While the IB program does fulfill many elements of the high school graduation requirements; these requirements vary from state to state, so there may often be certain classes or standards that you must complete to receive your high school diploma.

Your teachers and coordinators should make you aware of what you need to do, so it is usually not a big deal - just something to keep in mind.

Matriculation & Requirements

While the requirements for graduating high school vary, the standards for receiving an IB diploma do not.

Points

As a whole, you can earn up to 45 points towards an IB diploma.

Three of these points can come from the extended essay and TOK, the rest come from each course taken. Most people do not score 45 points; in general, it takes a total score of 24 or above to receive a diploma.

To receive an IB diploma, every candidate must complete the Extended Essay, CAS requirements, and TOK.

The extended essay and TOK paper are scored on a scale of A (highest) to E (lowest). In order to receive a diploma, a candidate MUST score at least a D on one of the papers.

If both papers are scored E, this is a failing condition and you will not receive a diploma regardless of any other course work.

If you do well, the TOK paper and extended essay can contribute up to 3 extra points towards the total diploma score.

Additionally, every candidate must complete six IB courses, one from each subject group though a group 6 (The Arts) course may be substituted by a class from another subject group.

At least three, and not more than four, of these courses must be taken at the higher level. Two to three are taken at the standard level.

Scoring

Each course is numerically evaluated on a scale from 1 to 7. This score comes from combination of the internal and external assessment scores. The weighting and components of each courses' assessment differs and you can check on the exact scoring for each class in chapter 3.

In order to receive a diploma: candidates must not score a grade

1 on any subject or have more than any three courses in which they score a grade 3.

Depending on which classes a candidate takes, there are several scoring minimums that must be met in order to matriculate. If any of these requirements are not met, a candidate will not receive a diploma **regardless** of their other scores.

If a candidate's overall score is below 27 they must:

- Gain at least 12 points in HL subjects and 9 in SL subjects if taking 3 HL courses.

- Gain at least 16 points in HL subjects and 6 in SL subjects if taking 4 HL courses.

- Not have score lower than a grade 3 at any HL subject.

- Not have more than one SL course for which they score a grade 2.

If a candidate's overall score is above 27, they must:

- Gain at least 11 points in HL subjects and 8 in SL subjects if taking 3 HL courses.

- Gain at least 14 points in HL subjects and 5 in SL subjects if taking 4 HL courses.

- Not have more than one HL course for which they score a grade 2.

- Not have more than two SL courses for which they score a grade 2.

Realistically, 24 points to pass means that you need to score an average grade of four in each of your IB courses, assuming that you do not receive any of the extra credit from the extended essay or TOK.

If you only achieve the minimums that are laid out above, then you will not receive a diploma.

Candidates do skate by with scores of 3 and 2 in a few classes; however it is best to avoid scoring that low in ANY subject if you can help it. Ideally, you want sevens in every class; though aiming for an average score of five or 6 will give you the best shot at getting your diploma.

Certificates

In the case that a candidate does not successfully receive a diploma, they will receive certificates indicating the grades that they received in each specific class as well as the extended essay, TOK, and CAS; if completed.

Getting your Scores

After your IB exams are completed in May, you will most likely graduate in June. By this point, you will have most likely already been accepted to a college and will be preparing for the next step of your academic life. However, IB scores, unlike class grades do not come out on your report card in June.

Your IB course scores are usually available to your program coordinator on the 5th of July, and are released the next day at noon on the 6th of July to candidates. (November exam scores come out the 5th and 6th of January)

Results are released online at **http://results.ibo.org** and are accessed using your candidate ID and a PIN, which you will get from your program coordinator.

Predicted Grades

A big part of the matriculation process is the predicted grade. A predicted grade is a grade that teachers will assign each student in their course before they take the final examination.

These grades are used in grade award meetings by IB evaluators to ensure the appropriateness of the final awarded grades. As well, the predicted grades are a way to evaluate the grade distributions and teaching in a particular subject.

In general, predicted grades are only seen by the subject teacher and the IB, however some schools may decided to release the predicted grades to students. In this case, a predicted grade can be a huge help before an exam. It will let you know how you are doing and what subjects you need to work on.

Do not let a predicted grade go to your head. Just because you scored well on a practice test does not mean that you will do well on the actually examination. If you receive a high predicted grade, take it as a compliment, and keep studying.

Remarking and Retesting

Sometimes, things just go wrong. For many students, a single point has meant the difference between receiving a diploma or getting certificates. If you worked hard for every subject, but did not quite make it, you may still have options.

If the grade received did not merit the work that was done for an external assessment and you suspect that the assessment was not correctly marked, your program coordinator may request an enquiry upon the results.

In this case, the candidate will pay a fee and the material will be thoroughly reassessed. This is a positive reassessment and can only lead to a higher grade in the course, not a lower one.

For external assessments, candidates are permitted to sit for a maximum of three examination sessions in each subject. This includes the first time that the test is taken.

If you failed to receive your diploma the first time, especially if you were only a few points away, than this is a viable option.

Retesting can occur during any of the scheduled examination sessions so if you mess up in May, you can retake a test to get your diploma in November.

If you do decided to retest, know that you will have to pay for the examination again, and probably study a lot harder that the first time around. For more details on retesting, talk to your IB coordinator.

What to do afterwards

Graduating high school can be one of the scariest and most liberating times of your life. Things are not so clear-cut, there is no definite path. Yet, at the same time, a world of opportunity will lie before you.

Use this time to your advantage. A lot of students will decide to go to college right away, beginning classes less than 3 or 4 months after they finish with high school and IB.

This may not always be the best plan. You have just come out through two grueling years of hard work, academic sweat, stress, blood, and tears.

Rushing back into everything right away can be overwhelming and de-motivating.

I agree that it is important to not lose your edge and a university education is almost essential in today's society. However, there are other options to consider before jumping immediately back into the fray.

One of the best options I have seen is to defer your enrollment into college. Differed enrollment means that you are accepted to a university, but you do not have to start going there right away.

This gives the security of being accepted along with the freedom of not having to go to school immediately 3 months after you graduate high school. Some people work, while others travel or volunteer in their time off.

Not only does this look good on a resume, it can help give you focus and motivation instead of the burnout that many college freshmen feel.

Finally, college is the right thing to do. Going to university not only teaches life skills, higher education is essential to starting most modern careers. Moreover, IB provides the perfect preparation for the demands of a university curriculum.

Whatever you do, look for what makes you happy and take the time to travel and discover what brings your joy and fulfillment.

Do not do things just because. Do them for the right reasons, your reasons, and you will find that the IB and life to be rewarding and fulfilling each step of your journey.

Appendix

Every end is a new beginning

-Unknown

Glossary of IB Terms

A selected list of terms in IB. Some you may know, some you may not. Learn a few and drop them during class to appear smart and witty.

Assessment Criteria: The specific criteria which is used to evaluate an assessment. The subjects which are tested during an assessment.

Bilingual Diploma: The diploma received when a student completes the IB in more than one primary language. In order to receive a bilingual diploma, candidates must complete Language A2 as well as several other IB courses in a secondary language.

Bullshit: To fake it. Eloquent and insincere rhetoric which disguises that you actually know very little or do not know what to say at all. Use as a last resort when writing papers and giving presentations. Often abbreviated as B.S.

Candidate: A student who is working towards their IB diploma.

Cardiff: A town in the UK where the IB has a large exam evaluation and course development center. Many of the assessments you complete are sent here including the extended essay.

CAS: Creativity, Action, and Service. The community service/action component of the IB diploma designed to apply lessons from the diploma program outside of the classroom.

Certificate: What IB students who do not complete a full diploma receive. Certificates indicate courses completed and grades received.

Coordinator: The IB coordinator is a position at every IB world school usually held by a teacher involved in the program. The coordinator is responsible for all official communication with the IB as well as organizing courses, exams, and all other aspects of the diploma program. Notoriously busy and stressed out.

Core Requirements: The Extended Essay, Theory of Knowledge and CAS,; three core components you must complete in order to receive an IB diploma. Usually worked on outside of normal class time.

Diploma Candidate: A students who is in the IB program working towards a full diploma.

Diploma Programme: The IB curriculum that makes up the IB diploma. Programme is a British spelling of program. Often shortened to DP.

Dossier: An organized file or collection of documents relevant to one particular subject.

EE: The Extended Essay research project. One of the three core requirements for the IB diploma. A 5,000 word essay describing the self-designed and constructed extended essay research project.

External Assessment : An IB examination that is graded (assessed) by official IB graders around the world. Usually composes 70-80% of the course grade.

Full Diploma: The complete IB diploma program. Includes six HL and SL courses as well as three core subject requirements.

Geneva: The global headquarters of the IB in Geneva, Switzerland.

Handbook of Procedures: A complex and thorough guide which describes every aspect of the diploma program. Used by program coordinators, it is completely digital. Formerly known as the Vade Macum.

Higher Level (HL): An IB course taught at the higher level lasts for two years and covers standard level material for the particular subject at a greater depth as well as additional material not covered by an SL course. HL courses are more difficult and have more (and longer) examination papers than SL courses. Diploma candidates must complete 3-4 HL courses.

IB (aka IBO): The International Baccalaureate. Non-governmental organization based in Geneva, Switzerland which organizes educational curriculum in schools around the world. Formerly called as the International Baccalaureate Organization, or IBO.

Instructor/Teacher: Someone who teaches or leads and IB course.

Internal Assessment: An IB examination that is completed in class and graded by the teacher. Usually a collection of work done during the course, a large project, or an oral assessment. Worth 20-30% of the course grade.

Invigilator (Supreme Prime Invigilator): He who watchs and muses while you sit for examinations. The examination moderator.

Learning Objectives: What the course aims to teach. What you are expected to learn during the course. Often these objectives are directly correlated to the material on the assessment for a particular subject.

Mark Scheme: A listing of the assessment criteria for a particular examination. Contains each specific item which you are graded on as well as a scale to help fairly evaluate your performance for each item.

Marks: Grades or points scored during an examination. British terminology.

Matriculate: To be recognized as working towards a degree or diploma.

Oral Assessment/Activity: An assessment which consists of the candidate speaking. May be a presentation, an interview, or a critical response to a particular text or other academic stimulus. Usually recorded for later evaluation.

Outside language: IB courses in one of the twenty or more languages that are available, though not normally offered in IB programs. Usually available only by special arrangement.

Paper: A writing assignment which is graded. A component of an IB external assessment. Usually, the external assessment for each subject will consist of several papers.

Pre-IB: Honors or advanced classes taken by students who want to attempt an IB diploma in the 1-2 years of high school before they start the IB program.

Prescribed List of Authors (PLA): A reading list that is used to select literature for Group 1 courses.

Prescribed Literature in Translation (PLT): A reading list of literature that has been translated. Used to select literature for Group 1 and Group 2 courses.

Primary Language: Your mother tongue. The language in which you take most IB courses including Language A1.

Prior Knowledge: For mathematics classes. Topics you are supposed to already know before starting a course or sitting for an examination. If the prior knowledge for a math course seems to difficult, consider taking an easier course.

Secondary Language: A foreign language, or a language other than that taken for Language A1. Any group 2 course is taught in a secondary language.

Standard Level (SL): An IB course taught at the standard level lasts for one year and usually only covers the basic aspects of a subject. Diploma candidates must take 2-3 SL courses.

Subject Group: Six core areas that are covered in the diploma program:

Group 1: Primary Language
Group 2: Secondary Language
Group 3: Individuals and Societies (Social Sciences)
Group 4: Experimental Sciences
Group 5: Mathematics & Computer Science
Group 6: The Arts

Subject Outline: An overview of the topics covered in a course. The official published IB syllabus for a course.

Target Language: The language in which a course is taught. Usually applies to group 2 courses.

The IB Hexagon: A hexagonal diagram which visually represents the structure of the diploma program.

Sit for an Exam: To take a test or IB examination. British terminology.

TOK: The Theory of Knowledge class. One of the three core requirements for the IB diploma. A practical and philosophical exploration of what knowledge is and what it means to know.

Unseen Passage: A selection of text which a candidate has never seen before and must critically evaluate for an examination in language A1 courses.

Vade Macum: The thick and complex handbook for IB coordinators which covers every aspect of the diploma program. Currently called the IB Handbook of Procedures and are completely digital.

Works: A text or other piece of writing which is studied during an IB course. Usually refers to books, poems, and other pieces of literature studied in the Language A1 course.

World School:Any school which is officially allowed to offer the IB diploma program or IB classes is designated as an IB World School.

Command Terms

Command Terms are terms used in IB examinations. While some of the words seem benign, they each have a specific meaning and how well a response meets the requirements of a given term is often critical in determining the mark given.

Analyze: Break down in order to bring out the essential elements or structure.

Comment: Give a judgment based on a given statement or result of a calculation.

Compare: Give an account of the similarities between two (or more) items or situations, referring to both (all) of them throughout.

Compare and contrast: Give an account of similarities and differences between two (or more) items or situations, referring to both (all) of them throughout.

Contrast: Give an account of the differences between two (or more) items or situations, referring to both (all) of them throughout.

Describe: Give a detailed account.

Discuss: Offer a considered and balanced review that includes a range of arguments, factors or hypotheses. Opinions or conclusions should be presented clearly and supported by appropriate evidence.

Evaluate: Make an appraisal by weighing up the strengths and limitations.

Examine: Consider an argument or concept in a way that uncovers the assumptions and interrelationships of the issue.

Explain: Give a detailed account including reasons or causes.

Explore: Undertake a systematic process of discovery.

Interpret: Use knowledge and understanding to recognize trends and draw conclusions from given information.

Investigate: Observe, study, or make a detailed and systematic examination, in order to establish facts and reach new conclusions.

Justify: Give valid reasons or evidence to support an answer or conclusion.

To what extent: Consider the merits or otherwise of an argument or concept. Opinions and conclusions should be presented clearly and supported with appropriate evidence and sound argument.

Command Terms courtesy of the International Baccalaureate Organization

Timeline of the IB Diploma Program

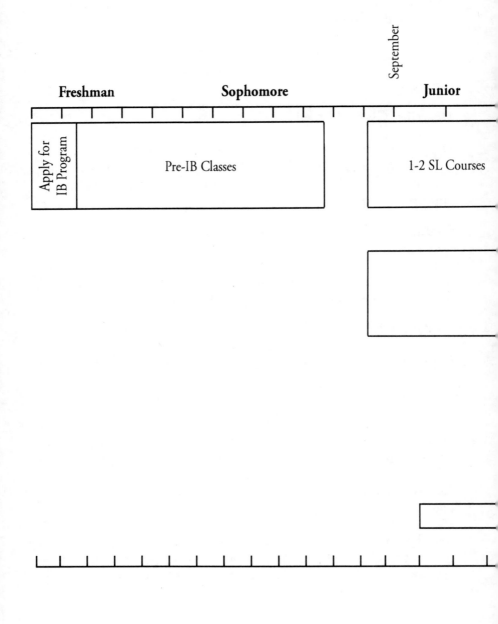

September

| Freshman | Sophomore | Junior |

Apply for IB Program

Pre-IB Classes

1-2 SL Courses

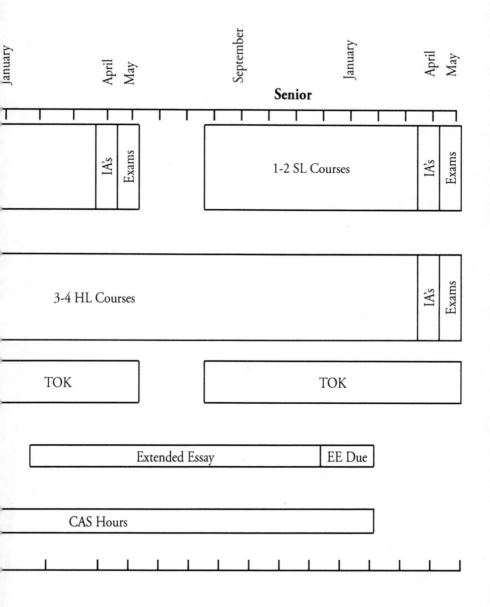

Languages in IB

Available course languages for 2010

While IB has offered courses in over 70 languages, the majority of classes are taught in English, French, or Spanish.

While courses from groups 1 and 2 have the most language selection.

Language A1

For May examinations, there are 44 available languages:

Amharic	English	Korean	Filipino	Swahili
Arabic	Finnish	Latvian	Polish	Swedish
Bosnian	French	Lithuanian	Portuguese	Thai
Bulgarian	German	Macedonian	Russian	Turkish
Catalan	Hebrew	Malay	Serbian	Welsh
Chinese	Hindi	Modern	Sesotho	
Croatian	Hungarian	Greek	Sinhalese	
Czech	Indonesian	Nepali	Slovak	
Danish	Italian	Norwegian	Slovene	
Dutch	Japanese	Persian	Spanish	

For November examinations, there are 2 **additional** languages offered:

Afrikaans   Siswati SL

Language B

For May examinations, there are 20 available languages:

Arabic	Finnish	Indonesian	Norwegian
Cantonese	French	Italian	Portuguese
Danish	German	Japanese	Russian
Dutch	Hebrew SL	Korean	Spanish
English	Hindi	Mandarin	Swedish

For November examinations, there is 1 **additional** language offered: Siswati SL

Ab-Initio SL

For May & November examinations, there are 10 available languages:

Arabic	Malay
French	Mandarin
German	Russian
Italian	Spanish
Japanese	Swahili

Diploma Checklist

Use this checklist to plan your classes and ensure that you receive a diploma.

See chapters 3 & 4 for detailed information on courses.

Courses

1. Choose **one** of the following options:

   ☐ 3 HL & 3 SL Courses

   - Score 12 points in HL courses (minimum avg. score of 4)
   - Score 9 points in SL courses (minimum avg. score of 3)

   ☐ 4 HL & 2 SL Courses

   - Score 16 points in HL courses (minimum avg. score of 4)
   - Score 6 points in SL courses (minimum avg. score of 3)

2. Complete (at least) one course from each subject group:

   ☐ Group 1 (Primary Language)
   ☐ Group 2 (Secondary Language)
   ☐ Group 3 (Individuals and Societies)
   ☐ Group 4 (Experimental Sciences)
   ☐ Group 5 (Mathematics & Computer Science)
   ☐ Group 6 (The Arts)

Core Requirements

☐ Theory of Knowledge
   - Score a 'D' or above

☐ Extended Essay
   - Score a 'D' or above

☐ CAS
   Complete the learning objectives for each segment:

   ☐ Creativity
   ☐ Action
   ☐ Service

Scoring Worksheet: to help keep track of your progress. For more information on scoring, see page170.

First Year SL courses

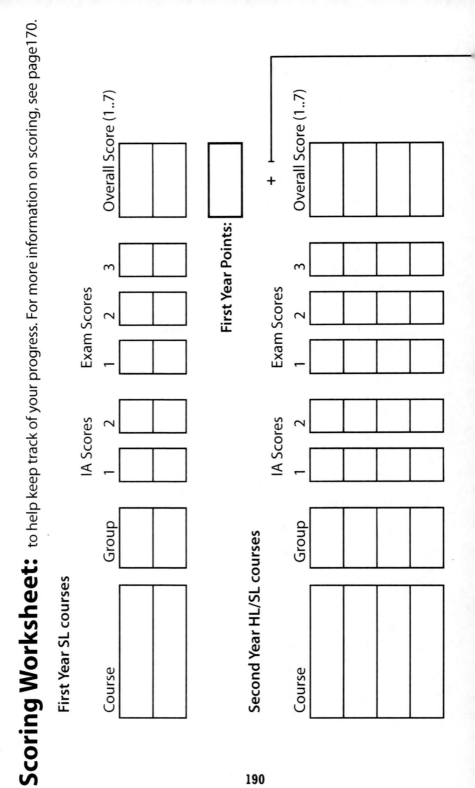

Course

Group

IA Scores
1   2

Exam Scores
1   2   3

Overall Score (1..7)

First Year Points:

Second Year HL/SL courses

Course

Group

IA Scores
1   2

Exam Scores
1   2   3

+

Overall Score (1..7)

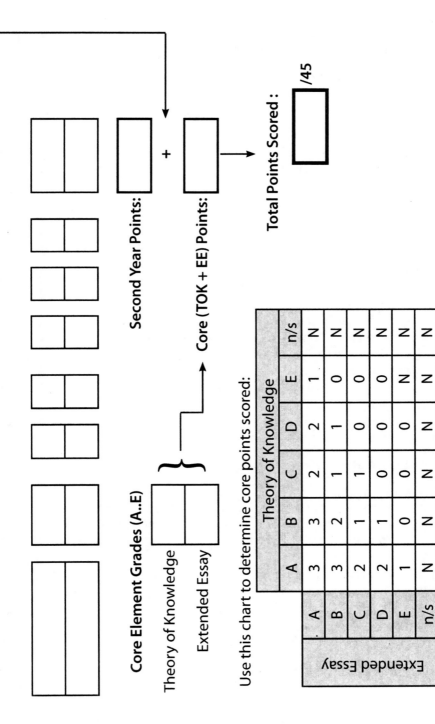

Internet Resources

Selected resources for all aspects of the diploma program. Check out www.survivetheib.com/links for more links & information.

Research and data

en.wikipedia.org
> Where to begin when you need to know anything about anything.

www.wolframalpha.com
> Amazing calculators and data aggregation. Will calculate anything from the square-root of pi to the gravitation acceleration in Seattle, Wa.

www.jstor.org
> Repository for thousands upon thousands of scholarly journal articles.

http:// infomine.ucr.edu/
> A comprehensive virtual library and reference tool for academic and scholarly internet resources

www.gale.cengage.com/psm
> Primary Source Microfilm and Scholarly Resources

www.google.com
> When you need to find it: start looking with the most comprehensive search engine on the internet.

Plagiarism

www.turnitin.com
> Used by many schools to check papers and projects for plagarism. With over 2 billion pages of web content and 100 million student papers on file, turnitin.com makes any sort of plagarism utterly impossible.

www.writecheck.com
> A version of turnitin.com for students that lets you check your paper for errors before you turn it in.

www.plagiarism.org
> Resources and information on plagiarism.

Diploma Program Specific

www.IBO.org
> The official web site of the International Baccalaureate.

www.managebac.com
> A new way for schools to digitally manage the IB program. Organizes your projects, papers, classes, exams, and everything else IB online.

Studying and Exam Prep

www.angelfire.com/wizard/ib-notes
> An amazing collection of links for notes for IB courses. Some links outdated, though still a great resource.

http://kstruct.com/ib_notes/Main_Page
> Great wiki page with updated IB course notes.

www.osc-ib.com/
> OSC publishes exam study guides and revision courses for the IB exams each year. Worth checking out if you need some additional practice.

http://ukcatalogue.oup.com/category/education/international/ibdiploma.do
> Oxford University Press' collection of study guides for the IB diploma.

Google

To use these tools, you need to have a google account which links them all together. They allow you to check email messages, write, store, and print documents, and organize your time from anywhere.

- mail.google.com (aka: gmail.com)
- docs.google.com
- calendar.google.com

Organization

www.todoist.com
> Hands down the best free task list manager on the internet. Simple and easy to use.

www.rememberthemilk.com
> Another free task list manager. Can be linked to twitter and your cell phone if you really need to remember to do something.

www.evernote.com
> A fantastic way to organize your research and thoughts. Keep all of your notes together and organized. Also has a Firefox extension that lets you 'clip' web pages as you surf for review later.

CPSIA information can be obtained at www.ICGtesting.com
Printed in the USA
LVOW130351090612

285309LV00022B/83/P